THE LIBRARY
ST. MARY'S COLLEGE OF MARYLAND
ST. MARY'S CITY, MARYLAND 20686

Enrique A. Laguerre

Twayne's World Authors Series

Luis Dávila, Editor of Puerto Rican Literature
Indiana University, Bloomington

TWAS 646

ENRIQUE A. LAGUERRE

*For Manuel,
and to the memory of Manuel Irizarry Gallardo,
who always carried Puerto Rico in his heart.*

Contents

About the Author
Preface
Chronology

> *Chapter One*
> A Lucid Conscience   1
>
> *Chapter Two*
> A Great Latin American Novel   9
>
> *Chapter Three*
> Apotheosis of the Jíbaro: *Montoya Plantation*   24
>
> *Chapter Four*
> Two Solitary Lives   42
>
> *Chapter Five*
> An Important Period of History   58
>
> *Chapter Six*
> The Wandering Puerto Rican   77
>
> *Chapter Seven*
> Who Am I? The Problem of Identity   93
>
> *Chapter Eight*
> Full Circle and Beyond: *Benevolent Masters*   109
>
> *Chapter Nine*
> Theater, Short Stories, and Essays   125
>
> *Chapter Ten*
> Summary and Conclusions   145

Notes and References   151
Selected Bibliography   157
Index   162

About the Author

Estelle Irizarry, professor of Spanish and Spanish-American literature at Georgetown University, holds the B.A. degree from Montclair State College, the M.A. from Rutgers University, and the Ph.D. from George Washington University.

Professor Irizarry is the author of *Teoría y creación literaria en Francisco Ayala* (Madrid: Editorial Gredos, 1971); *La inventiva surrealista de E. F. Granell* (Madrid: Ínsula, 1976); *Francisco Ayala* (Boston: Twayne Publishers, 1977); *Rafael Dieste* (Boston: Twayne Publishers, 1979); *La broma literaria en nuestros días* (New York: Eliseo Torres, 1980), and *La creación literaria de Rafael Dieste* (La Coruña: Ediciós do Castro, 1980). She has prepared annotated critical editions of Francisco Ayala's *El rapto, Fragancia de jazmines y Diálogo entre el amor y un viejo* (Barcelona: Editorial Labor, 1974), the Argentine classic *Martín Fierro* by José Hernández (Zaragoza: Clásicos Ebro, 1975), and *Versos de una . . .* by César Tiempo (Buenos Aires: Editorial Rescate, 1977).

Professor Irizarry has written a monthly section on Hispanic culture in the United States for the Mexican magazine *Nivel* since 1970 and has contributed many studies of Spanish and Spanish-American literature to scholarly journals, such as *Ínsula, Cuadernos Hispanoamericanos, Cuadernos Americanos, Papeles de Son Armadans, La Torre, Espiral,* and *Inti.* She has also written chapters in several volumes of collective criticism published in Spain, Mexico, and the United States.

Preface

The purpose of this book is to provide readers of English with a critical analysis of the works of Enrique A. Laguerre, Puerto Rico's master novelist whose dedication to his art spans more than forty years. Since 1935, when Laguerre came into the forefront of Puerto Rican fiction with the publication of *La llamarada* [The Blaze], several generations of Puerto Ricans have read his works, which in successive editions have been appreciated by both sophisticated scholars and humble folk, adults and students of the island's schools. His novels, however, have been accorded rather limited critical attention outside of Puerto Rican circles, although they are no more—or less—regional than those of most other Latin American writers. While it is difficult to speculate on the reasons for this, since I feel his works deserve such attention, it is significant to note that Laguerre has always maintained a low profile, avoiding political pronouncements, personal promotions, and literary cliques. Although he has traveled outside the island, he has carried out his writing career from his particular corner of the world, which happens to be Puerto Rico. He expresses himself in the pages of his novels and other writings, in the classroom, in the media via his weekly essays in *El Mundo,* and in lectures, but always motivated by public service and not professional expediency. Despite the fame he enjoys in Puerto Rico, where his name is familiar to anyone who can read, he is as accessible to his public as a good teacher is to his students.

Since the author's reputation rests primarily on his achievements as a novelist, major attention has been directed toward his work in this genre. My intention has been to uncover conscious and perhaps unconscious motivations that may have influenced the creative process, supporting my conclusions with examples and, when possible, documentation. To this effect I have not hesitated to employ imagination and intuition in the service of more conventional logical procedures, for art does not always yield its secrets to a purely intellectual approach and should, I think, stimulate creative response that is appropriate to the spirit of the work. Aware of the highly charged political and intellectual

ENRIQUE A. LAGUERRE

climate which exists in Puerto Rico, I have tried to maintain a dispassionate attitude and have made every attempt to extract meanings and implications which I feel may be legitimately derived from the text. Laguerre, faithful to his own lucid conscience, has steadily conserved his individual criteria and personal integrity as a writer and as a Puerto Rican; he serves no political cause or interest groups with his pen, and I have tried to respect this attitude on his part.

The method of analysis is inductive, allowing each work studied to suggest its own particular focus or mode of interpretation based on its content and internal demands. While not pretending to be exhaustive, I have endeavored to point out in each work studied major orientations, real events which are fictionalized, and narrative techniques and structures. Any one of these aspects certainly invites further critical study. An additional perspective attempts to view Laguerre's writings as a unified corpus, noting interrelations between individual works and reiterated techniques as well as changes in the evolution of his fiction.

I have tried to maintain a balance between Puerto Rican themes and universal ones, in consonance with that which the author's works imply. Laguerre's novels, in accordance with the spirit of his literary generation, that of the 1930s, reflect the growth of Puerto Rico's awareness of its cultural and historical identity during the past hundred years; his protagonists' individual destinies are entwined with those of the community to which they belong, so that historical, social, and political events are explained when relevant to the analysis. Laguerre, however, sees the Puerto Rican also as an inhabitant of the world and the concerns present in his fictions are largely shared by twentieth-century man in general—alienation, confusion, and the search for authentic values—and to this effect, universal allusions and implications will be pointed out. As a professor of literature and as a critic, the novelist is very much aware of changing trends in Latin American literature; his early interest in the world of legends and myths anticipates some of the innovations now recognized as characteristic of the so-called "New Narrative." His fiction reveals the major currents of Latin American literature during the last forty years: regional, social, magical, and experimental.

Artistic elaboration is not considered here as an end in itself, so that imagery, symbolism, and diverse stylistic devices are treated in relation to the effects they produce in complementing the content.

Preface

Since the bibliography on Laguerre is extensive, including nearly 2,000 entries—largely reviews—reference is made in textual discussion only to those considered most relevant to the analysis. This is the first monograph on Laguerre to be published in English and the only one which focuses upon each work as a whole rather than on specific aspects or characters. Translations of titles and passages, except for *The Labyrinth* and *Benevolent Masters*, are mine. It is hoped that this volume will stimulate further translations of the author's works and will contribute to enhancing his image as a universal author as well as a Puerto Rican writer.

Estelle Irizarry

Georgetown University

Chronology

1906	May 3: Born in Aceituna section of the town of Moca, Puerto Rico, one of eight children of Juan Z. Laguerre and Atanasia Vélez.
1912	Begins primary grades in Isabela.
1916	Moves to Aguadilla to attend school.
1924	Graduates high school and takes a teaching course.
1925	Begins teaching in Moca.
1926	Undertakes studies at the University of Puerto Rico on Saturdays and during the summer.
1927	Receives certification as a teacher.
1935	Publishes *La llamarada* [The Blaze], immediately acclaimed by the critics.
1936	Receives the Normal School diploma with high honors. *The Blaze* is honored by the Institute of Puerto Rican Literature. Director at a Second Unit School in Moca, Puerto Rico.
1937	Is awarded bachelor's degree in education at the University of Puerto Rico with high honors and the Menéndez Pidal medal for excellence in philology.
1937–1938	Teaches at Fajardo High School.
1938–1941	Prepares instructional programs at School of the Air.
1941	Is awarded the master of arts degree at the University of Puerto Rico, presenting his thesis, *La poesía modernista en Puerto Rico*. Begins teaching at the university and writes texts for the Department of Education. Publishes *Solar Montoya* [Montoya Plantation].
1943	*El 30 de febrero* [The 30th of February].

1944 *La resentida* [The Resentful Woman] staged by the University Theater. Marries Beatriz Saavedra.

1947 His wife dies.

1949 *La resaca* [The Undertow]. Goes to New York to study for the doctorate at Columbia University until 1951. Sends articles to *El Diario de Puerto Rico* under the pseudonym Luis Uroyán.

1951 Returns from trip to Europe and goes to Mexico to work for UNESCO on an education project in Pátzcuaro. Publishes *Los dedos de la mano* [The Fingers of the Hand].

1952 Begins weekly radio program, *Puntos de partida* [Points of Departure], which is a precedent for the 1959 "Hojas libres" [Free Pages] in *El Mundo*.

1954 Founds the magazine *Paliques* with Domingo Marrero, Julio Marrero Núñez, and Samuel de la Rosa.

1955 Appointed to the Board of Directors of the Institute of Puerto Rican Culture.

1956 *La ceiba en el tiesto* [The Ceiba Tree in the Flower Pot] and *Pulso de Puerto Rico* [Pulse of Puerto Rico], the latter a selection of the radio program *Points of Departure* broadcast from 1952 to 1954.

1959 Publication of *El laberinto* [The Labyrinth]. Begins his weekly "Hojas libres" in *El Mundo*.

1960 *The Resentful Woman* published. English translation of *The Labyrinth* is published in New York.

1961 On sabbatical, travels to Mexico, Central America, Brazil, Uruguay, and Argentina.

1962 Travels to Spain. Publishes *Cauce sin río* [River Bed without a River].

1967 Elected president of the Society of Puerto Rican Authors.

1968 Member PEN Club in New York.

1969 *Honoris Causa* in Philosophy, Catholic University, Ponce, Puerto Rico. *La poesía modernista en Puerto Rico* [Modernist Poetry in Puerto Rico] published.

Chronology

1970   *El fuego y su aire* [Fire and Its Air]. Director of Hispanic Studies at the Catholic University in Ponce. Marries Luz Virginia Romero García.

1972   Is appointed president of the Board of Directors of the Institute of Puerto Rican Culture. Retires Emeritus from the University of Puerto Rico and is visiting Professor at City University of New York.

1973   Travels in South America.

1975   *Honoris Causa* in Philosophy, University of Puerto Rico. Travels to Spain.

1976   *Los amos benévolos* [Benevolent Masters].

1977   *Polos de la cultura iberoamericana* [Poles of Ibero-American Culture]. Trip to Brazil and Venezuela.

1980   Named Honorary Fellow, American Association of Teachers of Spanish and Portuguese.

Chapter One
A Lucid Conscience
Growing up in a Changing Puerto Rico

Enrique A. Laguerre was born May 3, 1906, the son of Juan Z. Laguerre and Atanasia Vélez, in the Aceituna section of the municipality of Moca. He was born eight years after Puerto Rico was ceded to the United States by Spain at the close of the Spanish American War, a change of sovereignty unforeseen by the Puerto Ricans, who had just gained governmental autonomy from Spain after a long, hard struggle against despotic rule. The mood of these times would later be reflected in Laguerre's only play, *La resentida* [The Resentful Woman], staged in 1944, which dramatizes the resentment caused by the Spanish government's persecution of Puerto Rican autonomists in "the terrible year of '87" which expresses itself eleven years later in acts of terrorism against Spanish ranchers and their families. It is not surprising that Laguerre often resorts to nature for the symbolism which abounds in his novels, for indeed nature itself sometimes suggests such symbolism, as in the case of the momentous trauma of 1898 after four centuries of Spanish rule followed the next year by a natural catastrophe, the great hurricane of San Ciríaco, which claimed 3,000 lives and inflicted heavy damages upon the island, beginning an almost symbolic pattern in which major events seem underscored by nature's upheavals.[1]

The young Enrique grew up in the mountainous terrain of his parents' coffee plantation, where he was greatly affected by the nature around him and by the humble country folk he would later bring to life in his novels. He had to walk some four kilometers each day in order to attend classes at a rural schoolhouse where as a result of the Americanization program English had been imposed as the exclusive language of instruction, to the dismay of many teachers who hardly mastered that tongue. The total population of the island then was approximately 1 million; Laguerre would see this number more than triple. In those early years there was a serious change in the Puerto Rican economy, particularly in his own region of the island, which the novelist would later treat in his first novels. American corporations valued the production of sugar over that of coffee, creating an imbalance which made life especially difficult for the Puerto Rican *jíbaro* or peasant. With the growth of sugar plantations and mills on the coast, large landed estates with absentee owners were formed with the corresponding abuses depicted in Laguerre's first novel, *La llamarada* [The Blaze, 1935]. The subsequent deterioration of coffee production in the mountain areas appears in his second novel, *Solar Montoya* [Montoya Plantation, 1941]. In both books the *jíbaro's* struggle with social and economic ills is compounded by natural disasters like the great hurricanes which periodically whip the island and whose names remain in the collective memory, often used as time references rather than years.

Laguerre found himself a United States citizen at eleven, when the Jones Law granted Puerto Ricans American citizenship, with all its rights and duties. Coinciding with the end of the First World War in 1918, severe earthquakes shook the island causing heavy casualties, especially in the western part of the island where Laguerre lived.

The author attended high school in the coastal city of Aguadilla, not far from Moca, where he began to write short pieces and, encouraged by the educator Carmen Gómez Tejera, took a course in teaching. Upon graduating from high school in 1924, he immediately embarked upon what would be a lifelong career in teaching which would take him to several island towns and different academic levels. Surely this experience, which began with teaching in an elementary school in the most mountainous section of his own community, provided him with valuable insights and helped to develop a natural gift for communicating with people on all levels, both humble folk and intellectuals. His novels have enough density and artistic elaboration to attract the most sophisticated reader, yet in their basic simplicity and narrative interest appeal also to the nonintellectual. Laguerre has been a favorite author of generations of Puerto Ricans; *The Blaze* alone has been published in some twenty editions since 1935 and is often read in public schools throughout the island, a very fitting tribute to an author who has always been a dedicated teacher. Perhaps too the great importance Laguerre accords to dialogue in his novels may be attributed to his fondness for the classroom dialogue of teaching.

The Making of a Novelist

While continuing to teach, Laguerre studied in the summers at the University of Puerto Rico, which had been founded only two years after he was born. His goal was to attain a degree in teaching.

The 1920s in Puerto Rico saw the advent of two opposing ideals which would continue to rock island politics; independence and statehood, as well as the continued growth of the Socialist movement, reflected in Laguerre's fifth novel, *Los dedos de la mano* [The Fingers of the Hand], in 1951. Again in some fateful way nature seemed to accompany the island's traumas, for in 1928 another destructive hurricane, San Felipe, wreaked havoc, as if to foreshadow the impending economic crisis of the Great Depression, which afflicted the island with particular cruelty, in spite of several federal programs set up to relieve the situation. Laguerre decided to attend classes at the University of Puerto Rico full time to complete his teaching degree. It was during this time, in 1935, that he published his first novel, *The Blaze,* which was instantly hailed as a major event by the critics and awarded a prize by the Institute of Puerto Rican Literature as the best work in its genre published in Puerto Rico since Manuel Zeno Gandía's excellent naturalistic novel *La charca* [The Mud Pool] of 1894. Laguerre also published critical reviews, essays, poems, and stories in the campus publication *Ámbito* and in the periodicals *Brújula* and *Ateneo Puertorriqueño*.

This was a period of intense political unrest, again symbolically heralded by a severe hurricane, San Ciprián, in 1932. The same year Laguerre received the Bachelor of Arts degree, a series of violent events erupted in the Ponce Massacre, a confrontation between Nationalist demonstrators and police which was followed by an unsuccessful attempt on the governor's life with the subsequent conviction of Nationalist leaders. Allusions to this political turmoil appear in Laguerre's novel *La ceiba en el tiesto* [The Ceiba Tree in the Flower Pot,

1956], but as is generally true in Laguerre's fiction, political events in themselves are not the main concern but are alluded to in the intrahistory of his characters. During this period an intellectual renovation was initiated by authors of the so-called Generation of the 1930s which became active after the demise of Modernism and the vanguard "isms" of the postwar era. Concha Meléndez situates in this generation those writers born between 1895 and 1910, largely influenced by their association with the University of Puerto Rico and the magazine *Índice,* founded by Antonio S. Pedreira, Alfredo Collado Martell, Vicente Géigel Polanco, and Samuel R. Quiñones.[2] Their writings were mostly essays, short stories, and occasionally novels, but the only member of the generation who cultivated the novel persistently, as Concha Meléndez observes, is Laguerre, for while bound by similar experiences and concerns, each writer followed a different direction in his creative expression. The following generation, that of the 1940s, is generally more pessimistic and defiant in its outlook toward the themes of national consciousness brought into the fore by the previous generation, deeply concerned with Puerto Rico's past and future.

After some time teaching in the Voladoras section of Moca, Laguerre returned to the university for certification to teach high school with specialization in Spanish language and literature. There he received the Menéndez Pidal medal for outstanding work in Hispanic philology. During this time he collaborated in the magazines *Hostos* and *Isla.* He then taught at Fajardo High School, writing for the production committee of the School of the Air of the Department of Public Instruction while continuing his studies for the Master of Arts degree. He distinguished himself with an oft-cited thesis entitled "La poesía modernista en Puerto Rico" [Modernist Poetry in Puerto Rico], presented before the Faculty of Hispanic Studies in 1941, roughly the same time that a new political party, the Popular Democrats, under the leadership of Luis Muñoz Marín, began to flourish amid promises to raise the quality of life in Puerto Rico. During this same period Laguerre published two more novels: *Solar Montoya* [Montoya Plantation, 1941] and *El 30 de febrero* [The 30th of February, 1943], the latter dealing with the life of a university student.

Laguerre's formative readings, according to Zayas Micheli, included periodicals such as the *Revista de las Antillas, Índice, Puerto Rico Ilustrado,* and *Álbum de Guayama,* where he read the early poetry of Luis

Palés Matos, a writer of "Negroide" poetry. In world literature he read the Bible (with preference for the Old Testament), Chateaubriand, Victor Hugo, Dostoevski, Chekhov, Balzac, Flaubert, Ibsen, Dickens, Gogol, Zola, Thackeray, the Goncourt brothers, Theodore Dreiser, Sinclair Lewis, Upton Sinclair, Clifford Odets, Erskine Caldwell, and Willa Cather, which obviously gave him an extensive acquaintance with social literature. In Hispanic literature besides reading the *Quijote*—which leaves its mark on every Spanish-language writer, and Laguerre is no exception as we shall see—he read the best of the flowering of the Spanish-American novel of regionalism, authors like Azuela, Gallegos, Güiraldes, and Rivera.[3] One of Puerto Rico's finest critics, Antonio S. Pedreira, proclaimed Laguerre's first novel, *The Blaze*, a "sister novel" to Rómulo Gallegos's *Doña Bárbara* (1929), *La vorágine* [The Whirlpool] by José Eustasio Rivera (1924), and Ricardo Güiraldes's *Don Segundo Sombra* (1926), and rightly so.[4] With time it became more customary to consider Laguerre in the almost exclusive context of Puerto Rican letters, but it is significant to note that early in his writing career, with *The Blaze* and *Montoya Plantation*, he was obviously attuned to the currents of Latin American literature, notably regionalism and the agrarian novel, to which he gave a particularly Puerto Rican character while emulating the "Criollista" novel of the land. This awareness of Spanish-American trends would continue to grow and manifest itself in his art, despite the thematic commitment to Puerto Rico.

Responsibility and Commitment of Adulthood

After receiving the M.A. degree, Laguerre began teaching at the University of Puerto Rico. His play *The Resentful Woman* was staged in 1944 and *La resaca* [The Undertow], a novel, was published in 1949 and very well received by the critics. He interrupted his teaching to work for a doctorate at Columbia University in New York from 1949 to 1951. This was followed by travels to Cuba and to Mexico, where he served as coordinator of the Regional Center of Basic Education for the UNESCO in Pátzcuaro, in the state of Michoacán, preparing reading texts for the educational program.

The 1950s saw the unprecedented flow of Puerto Ricans to the United States mainland, principally to industrial centers in hope of economic advancement, and to handle the influx, old World War II planes were outfitted as "aerobusses." Laguerre made several trips to the United States between 1952 and 1959, observing firsthand the experiences of the Puerto Ricans, unprepared for life in the urban centers, and portraying their feelings of alienation, disillusionment, and strangeness in contact with the new environment in his novels *La ceiba en el tiesto* [The Ceiba Tree in the Flower Pot, 1956], *El laberinto* (1959)—published soon after in translation as *The Labyrinth*—and in *Cauce sin río* [River Bed without a River, 1962]. He continued to publish articles, essays, and reviews in diverse Puerto Rican journals.

During these years important changes were also occurring within Puerto Rico, such as the naming of the first Puerto Rican governor in 1946, two years later the first election of governor, and in 1952 the establishment of the Estado Libre Asociado or Commonwealth. A vigorous campaign of economic development, "Operation Bootstrap," was launched to bring tourism and mainland business and industry to the island. The rapid rise of prosperity for a growing urban middle class brought a new range of problems of a moral and spiritual nature, as a more pragmatic ethos and increased American influence threatened to displace traditional values. These changes and their effects on the individual are treated in Laguerre's latest novels, *El fuego y su aire* [Fire and Its Air, 1970] and *Los amos benévolos* [Benevolent Masters, 1976].

In 1952 Laguerre assumed the directorship of the magazine *Presente,* together with the great Peruvian social novelist Ciro Alegría, who was then a visiting professor at the University of Puerto Rico. Laguerre was also a codirector of *Palique,* for which he wrote a section entitled "Summary of the Puerto Rican Intellectual Movement." In addition he penned a column called "Perspective" in *Artes y Letras* and another, "Hojas Libres" [Free Pages], in *El Mundo,* for which he received an award in 1960 from the Institute of Puerto Rican Literature and which he continues to write weekly. He transmitted a radio program of public information and criticism called "Points of Departure" from 1952 to 1959 for the government radio station WIPR. A selection of these broadcasts was published in 1956 as *Pulso de Puerto Rico* [Pulse of Puerto Rico]. In 1955 with the founding of the Puerto Rican Academy of the Spanish Language, he was elected to membership and joined the directorship of the Institute of Puerto Rican Culture, an agency dedicated to preserving Puerto Rican historical buildings and landmarks and to encouraging artistic and cultural programs of all kinds.

In 1961 and 1962 Laguerre traveled to Mexico, Central America, Panama, Brazil, Argentina, Uruguay, Italy, and Spain. In Madrid the publication of his novel *River Bed without a River* was marked by a reception in his honor. While in Brazil Laguerre studied the language and literature of that country, which he later taught at the University of Puerto Rico. After the fall of Trujillo he visited the Dominican Republic.

His teaching career continued at the Catholic University of Puerto Rico, where he planned a Caribbean Studies Program as director of the Department of Hispanic Studies. His *Complete Works* were published by the Institute of Puerto Rican Culture in 1962, 1964, and 1974. In 1967 Laguerre was elected president of the Society of Puerto Rican Authors. He was visiting professor at City University of New York from 1969 to 1970 and was granted an Honoris Causa doctorate from Catholic University and the University of Puerto Rico, from which he became Emeritus in 1970. Laguerre was president of the Board of Directors of the Institute of Puerto Rican Culture from 1972 to 1976.

The 1960s and 1970s brought tremendous changes to Puerto Rico in the form of increased income, immigration, and educational opportunities, and at the same time problems typical of an urban society largely dependent upon the United States. Laguerre has been a vigilant observer of the dramatic changes, seeing the agrarian society of his youth turn into a predominantly industrialized one, accompanied by both affluence and poverty and by crises of identity and of values, which in some respects may be considered peculiar to Puerto Rico and in others symptomatic of similar problems afflicting Latin American countries. There is an old Spanish proverb that states that "there is no evil that does not do some good" and that good may lie in the artistic achievements which come from writers of conscience capable of extracting universal significance from troubled times and transmuting them into art.

Through the years Laguerre has been adept at taking the "pulse of Puerto Rico," as he calls his book of essays, perceiving with great lucidity the changing face of concerns, some economic and others political, social, spiritual, or ethical. With the publication of his latest novels, *Fire and Its Air* and *Benevolent Masters,* Laguerre reveals his mastery of techniques associated with the so-called "New Latin American Narrative," but while his concerns are very Puerto Rican and at the same time universal, there is much in his writing which is distinctly Hispanic, and implicit in that is cultural affirmation.

Laguerre's narrative would seem to illustrate perfectly what Fernando Alegría has viewed as the fundamental change which has taken place in this century after the demise of the regional novel of the land: "The political emphasis on social criticism has yielded to the ethical projections of the conflicts narrated. The novelist of half century reacts as an individual before social contradictions, feels a personal responsibility and, before searching for the solution provided by parties, wants to extract the truth from the very depth of his conscience."[5]

While for the most part the great literary movements of the continent were late in coming to Puerto Rico, in this case it can be said that Laguerre was in the forefront of this emphasis upon ethical considerations based on independent criteria.[6] This is the impression one gleans from his 1943 novel *The 30th of February,* generally considered less favorably than his other novels, a narrative of transition, with its introspective examination of an individual who feels himself "an interim man." Laguerre has been a witness to profound changes in the society about him and, like Galdós in nineteenth-century Spain, he has set about to record them novelistically, responding to his circumstances affirmatively with his life and his responsible yet personal art.

Chapter Two
A Great Latin American Novel

The first part of the twentieth century saw the unprecedented success of outstanding Latin American novels, some of which attracted international attention. The most famous of these were *La vorágine* [The Whirlpool, 1924] by the Colombian writer José Eustasio Rivera, *Don Segundo Sombra* (1926) by the Argentine Ricardo Güiraldes, and *Doña Bárbara* (1929) by the Venezuelan Rómulo Gallegos. Fernando Alegría describes the general trend which these novels represented:

Every section of Hispanic America would come to have its own epic of man in ferocious struggle with nature and each one of these epics, whether in Brazil, in Venezuela, in Paraguay, in Guatemala, in Costa Rica, in Cuba or in Mexico carries within, the story of a defeat. The circumstances varied, but the background is unalterable: savage nature imposes itself upon man and the latter contributes to his own perdition refining the means of economic exploitation and homicide in the places he proposes to conquer.[1]

Enrique Laguerre's first novel, *La llamarada* [The Blaze], published in 1935, was quite obviously written under the inspiration and influence of the aforementioned novels. The well-known critic Antonio Pedreira immediately pointed out the family resemblance of this "sister novel," taking care not to diminish its importance as a national novel. It was clear that in *The Blaze* Puerto Rico had found its own great epic of nature and man, with all the artistic merit to distinguish it among those of other regions.

There are, of course, some important differences between Laguerre's novel and the others we have cited. As Pedreira noted, the Puerto Rican coastal landscape is decidedly different from the jungles of Colombia, the plains of Venezuela, or the pampa of the gaucho in Argentina. In addition, Laguerre anticipates some of the changes which subsequently would place more emphasis on the psychological penetration of the human protagonists and on the ethical projections of the struggle, two major factors which enriched the Latin American novel toward mid-century.[2]

The Blaze was enthusiastically received by prestigious critics like Concha Meléndez and Antonio Pedreira, although suggestions were made for simplification in the prose which the young novelist carried out in the revisions of the second edition which bore an excellent prologue by Pedreira, who states categorically, and with all the seriousness such a judgment implies, that *"The Blaze* is the best Puerto Rican novel written by a young Puerto Rican novelist in the contemporary period."[3] Over the years the novel has continued to delight readers in its many editions and has been read by generations of Puerto Rican students in the schools of the island. Recent criticism consistently upholds the early superlatives which the book elicited; Luis O. Zayas Micheli declared in 1974 that it represented a real "happening in the history of the Puerto Rican novel. Since *La charca* [The Mudpool], we hadn't had such a novel."[4]

Drama in the Cane Fields

In the opening part, entitled "Open Furrows," the narrator, who has overcome his sentimental attachment to Sarah to further his self-achieved career as a graduate agronomist, embarks upon his first job. Oscar "de" Mendoza (the "de" is a touch of presumption), the administrator of the Mill, introduces him to Don Florencio Rosado, supervisor of Palmares plantation bordering Santa Rosa, which the narrator—Juan Antonio Borrás—is to run. He stays at the old Spanish family home of the Alzamora sisters and their orphan niece Delmira. Their land, Santa Rosa, has been leased to the Mill. Juan Antonio feels exhilarated as he tours the plantation and meets his co-workers: Lope Corchado, head foreman of Santa Rosa, and Balbina Soltrén, a foreman of a group of peons, both of whom express contempt for the laborers. His impressions of others are decidedly more favorable: the centenarian Chelores; another landowner who leased his fields to the Mill—Juan Pablo Moreau—and his lovely daughter Pepiña; the Socialist Don Polo Cabañas, now confined to a wheel chair; and his dedicated son the carpenter Manuel, who asks Juan Antonio to find a job for a relative,

Segundo Marte. There are, however, some disquieting moments when Juan Antonio sees a peon with his teeth clenched, observes some miserable washerwomen, and converses with Don Polo about social inequality.

In "While the Cane Grows" Juan Antonio announces that he began this diary after an incident in which the laborer Ventura Rondón took ill in the cane field. He is appalled by the misanthropic Don Flor's lack of concern for the poor man and his numerous family. Juan Antonio sees Ventura Rondón's face multiplied throughout the fields and feels himself confronting Don Flor in a repetition of the traditional rivalry between the two plantations which many years before had led to a fatal "siege of the foremen."

A visit to the hovel of Rondón is convincing evidence of "the hair-raising defeat of these existences" (83) marred by hunger, illness, and poverty.[5] Conversations with Don Polo about socialism confirm Juan Antonio's own indignation, but he hesitates to do anything which may jeopardize the economic independence he worked so hard to achieve.

The third section, "Bad Weed," takes place in the cutting season. Juan Antonio is impressed by Don Polo's relative Segundo Marte, who seems too highly qualified to be seeking work in the cane fields. He attends the burial of Rondón and becomes aware of the abuses of holding back salaries, overcharging at the company store, and not supplying medical care. He too is part of this system, which he realizes devastates national pride and contributes to the moral, spiritual, and physical slavery of the jíbaro, or Puerto Rican peasant. A protest breaks out, led by Segundo, but it is all too quickly ended by the intervention of a Socialist leader, who speaks to the poverty-stricken workers from the running board of his automobile, and the Mediating Commission from San Juan. Juan Antonio avoids Don Polo to evade facing his own conscience and even collaborates with Don Oscar to undermine the provisions of the strike accord by underreporting the hours that the peons work, thus joining their general exploitation by politicians, business, and church.

In the third chapter, "Fire," Juan Antonio, still haunted by Don Polo's socialist ideas, is taken ill with fever under the hot sun of "the circle of fire" in the cane field. A hurricane rages, destroying property, crops, and people. Delmira, who had solicitously cared for Juan Antonio in his illness, is stricken with pernicious anemia. Juan Antonio decides his affection toward her is brotherly. He runs into the widow of Rondón, who supports her family by making moonshine. Don Flor is promoted and Juan Antonio takes charge of both plantations, moving to Palmares. Don Oscar, who uses the Palmares payroll to his own advantage, obliges him to lower the workers' salaries to save the Mill from problems with the American Sugar Co. Juan Antonio finds himself committing the same abuses he had censured in Don Flor and is falsely accused of informing on the Rondón widow. A new strike is brought to a speedy end by the San Juan Mediating Commission but fires break out in the fields and a peon is framed. Juan Antonio, suspecting that Segundo is behind the fires, stakes out one of the cane fields mentioned by an informer. After several nights of waiting with a guard, he surprises Segundo and though he achieves an advantage in the fight discards his pistol to fight man to man. Segundo, however, pulls a knife and, to save Juan Antonio from certain death, the guard shoots and kills Segundo. Juan Antonio becomes sullen and antisocial.

In the final chapter, "The Return," Don Oscar congratulates him for his zeal in defending the Mill, but Juan Antonio erupts in an angry tirade against the abuses sanctioned by the administrator. He visits the dying Don Polo and feels himself the object of collective hatred. Informed of the grave illness of his father, whose authoritarian decision to take him out of school made him leave home years before, he returns home in time to effect a reconciliation. Going back to Palmares to put things in order before a definitive departure, Juan Antonio finds a stinging, sarcastic letter of dismissal from the Mill and is replaced by an old classmate, who informs him of Sarah's unhappy marriage. Juan Antonio takes leave of Delmira, who later goes to a sanatorium in the capital; he proposes to Pepiña Moreau, who will follow him back to his native mountains, for "there one loves the land because the little plant produces and brings food to the peasant table" (231).

Puerto Rico's Own Novel

In his prologue to the second edition of *The Blaze* Pedreira asserts that Laguerre succeeds in creating an art which is genuinely rooted in Puerto Rican territorial spirit, following an aesthetic path which includes sociology and economy but goes beyond them. A more recent critic, Zayas Micheli, tries to prove the universality of Laguerre's fiction, feeling that the peculiar political situation of Puerto Rico has leaned toward a nationalistic approach. He correctly situates *The Blaze* in the author's "national cycle" because of its subject matter, but proceeds to point out particular aspects which may be considered universal. While it is evident that *The Blaze* is steeped in Puerto Rican ambience, even these local and distincly regional concerns need not be eliminated from a designation of universality. In *El fuego y su aire* [Fire and Its Air] Laguerre states: "There is water from our rivers in all the seas and in the clouds that rain over all the lands of the world. I am universal for having been born in some point on this earth."[6] Certainly *The Blaze* is as regional as *Doña Bárbara, Don Segundo Sombra,* and *Martín Fierro,* the Argentine epic, all of which have been translated into other languages and read by an international public while zealously considered national masterpieces. For Ortega y Gasset a great novel succeeds in "provincializing" the reader, in arousing his interest in the limited world presented: "To make every reader a 'transitory provincial' is, to my mind, the great secret of the novelist."[7] Indeed, the international reader may find pleasure in entering worlds different from his own, be they regional or fanciful, by the "travel" which reading affords. On the other hand, the national reader may not be as aware of his regional novel's universal appeal or projections. Zayas Micheli treats some of these in his book *Lo universal en Enrique A. Laguerre* [Universality in Enrique A. Laguerre].

For the international reader as well as for the Puerto Rican, *The Blaze* reproduces the reality of the sugar-cane plantations. The historical background is implicit in the novel but not explained; it is obvious only that there has been a change from "before" when the haciendas produced all their own needs. As the centenarian Chelores reflects, "Before we ate more plantains, drank more milk, ate more meat, though it was turtle. Now everything has changed. Milk in cans, meat in cans, beans in cans! Man, how disgusting!" (118). Slowly we realize with the protagonist that old landowners are being squeezed by taxes and the Mill run by absentee owners, the American Sugar Co., into leasing their lands, which are used for cultivation of a single crop that displaces others which served the jíbaro's needs. This is the economic situation that came about after the island was ceded to the United States, which placed a higher value on sugar than on coffee, the latter relegated to lands unfit for growing sugar.

The economic changes in turn give rise to social abuses, for there is no lack of Puerto Rican administrators to carry out the wishes of the Mill and collaborate with the absentee bosses. The demands of the Mill make it necessary to sacrifice the proletariat. Those in command are insensitive to the needs of the jíbaro workers totally dependent upon their policies. In this respect the face of Ventura Rondón which haunts Juan Antonio represents all the victims. The name Ventura, meaning luck, is ironic, for he and his large family are the epitome of luckless misfortune.

Laguerre also examines the psychology of the jíbaro in general and not just in a folkloric context. Jorge Luis Borges has indicated that every Argentine, no matter how urbane and sophisticated, has within him something of the gaucho Martín Fierro, and it may be equally maintained that every Puerto Rican retains something of the jíbaro. Laguerre seems to show that in order for there to be masters, there must be slaves, and the character of the jíbaro is collectively submissive, for, as Juan Antonio notes, the same machete which cuts the cane could be an instrument of rebellion. What is particularly interesting is that Juan Antonio Borrás shares the same defects he decries in the jíbaros he observes: lack of spirit or will to rebel against exploitation for fear of losing whatever they have. Like the essayist Antonio Pedreira in his book *Insularismo* he theorizes that this lassitude is in large measure an effect of the tropical climate.[8] When Juan Antonio proposes strengthening his will against all obstacles which stand in his way, he specifically avoids stepping into "the circle of fire" which saps the jíbaro's vitality. While theoretically convinced by Don Polo's defense of human rights and dignity, Juan Antonio can no more rebel against his masters than the poor jíbaro farm hands. Another jíbaro characteristic affecting his situation adversely is his intense individualism that may lead to machete duels but prevents effective collective action. Laguerre seems to suggest that this is not a racial quality, since the workers are a heterogeneous group of blacks, whites, yellows, and mestizos, although on one occasion Juan Antonio refers to the authentic jíbaro's color, whose pallor is a source of pride "and we forget his inanition, his anemia, his pain. It would be much better if we were a people who were stronger, more alert, happier, even though—what's the difference!—darker!" (200). Ironically, Juan Antonio, who reminds Don Flor that he is not far removed from the jíbaros he directs, does not realize that he too shares their weaknesses. He maintains a perspective of distance when he describes them, as if he were an outsider.

Social comment extends beyond the cane fields to other sectors of life such as the family, particularly paternal domination. Juan Antonio's father was not only a despot who wished to curtail his son's education but also a philanderer, as is the husband of Sarah, a custom which brings suffering to women and family.

Prominent in *The Blaze* is the depiction of customs, not idealized as in the Romantic tradition, but rather in varied shades of realism. We see the cultivation of sugar in all its stages and payday in the fields with the presence of the barber, traveling merchants, and vendors of native fruits and sweets. A description of a cockfight is not at all favorable, but a New Year's party and a dance at Ña Saturna's cabin provide an opportunity to reproduce several native songs and to recreate the atmosphere of the *bomba* (literally, "drum"), a dance of Afro-French origin popular in the coastal regions.

These *costumbrista* ("regional") scenes, more than attempts to create a native background for the reader, have an important purpose in the novel, for as Zayas Micheli indicates, Laguerre sees in tradition the authentic values which can restore vitality to the Puerto Rican; when Juan Antonio leaves Palmares he returns to the mountain because there the fountains of tradition remain. This may be qualified, however, for he only returns to the mountains when his father is dying, the autocrat whose Old World traditions inhibited the son, but whose Puerto Rican love for the land inspired him. Having made peace with his father and inheriting the land, Juan Antonio is free to follow his own road. Recalling that "the last Indian took refuge in the Yunque [mountain peak and rain forest, in the northeast] and died there with his gods," Juan Antonio also returns to the mountains, not to die but to "fight bravely against the ax, against the storms, against the invaders. We must not permit our individuals and our gods to die" (229). This return to "what is authentically ours" is postulated from the beginning of the novel, yet Juan Antonio's defense of tradition is selective and in many ways atavistic, with nostalgia for ways that are disappearing.

Chelores laments that "the dances of the past are ending. The bomba nowadays isn't what it used to be. The Negro has stopped being Negro; sometimes he is whiter than the white man in his ways" (209). Juan Antonio feels some ambivalence toward the past. Modern in the sense that he is a graduate agronomist dedicated professionally to the implantation of new and successful methods of cultivation, he is sensitive to tradition: "Why this anxiety that drags me to live in the past as if I had been born in another era? There are moments in which living in the present seems uphill!" (158). His contradictions are not fully resolved in the novel; his return to the mountain is also uphill and he must make his own life, strengthened by his "atavistic" ties toward cultural and religious traditions. Laguerre will continue to examine this problem of "what is authentically ours" in other novels, but there is no question that in *The Blaze* Puerto Rico found its own great epic of man and nature.

Nature and the Land

As we have noted, the agrarian theme and predominance of nature link *The Blaze* to tendencies popular in Latin America at that time. There is also similarity between Laguerre's novel and *La barraca* [The Cabin, 1898] by the Spanish author Vicente Blasco Ibáñez, a regional portrayal of agrarian customs in Valencia in which fire becomes an expression of collective hate and revenge, although Blasco's style and Naturalistic orientation are far from our author's way of writing. Laguerre's novel is a Puerto Rican contribution to the distinctively Latin American theme of "civilization versus barbarity," a theme expounded by the Argentine author Domingo Faustino Sarmiento in his book *Civilización y barbarie: Vida de Juan Facundo Quiroga* [Civilization and Barbarity: Life of Juan Facundo Quiroga] in 1845 and symbolized most effectively in Gallegos's *Doña Bárbara*. Laguerre's treatment of the theme, however, contributes a new and paradoxical view in which civilization is the source of barbarism, and not nature. Juan Antonio, for example, recoils from the conventional trappings and hypocritical formulas of society and sees in nature a repository of spiritual values: "We live dying in the vicious circle of falsities—luxuries, vanities, trifles—and we avoid that which elevates us. How much more value there is in understanding the joy of a small blue flower than mounting the most luxurious car!" (205). This is reiterated throughout the novel.

One of the most outstanding aspects of nature in *The Blaze* is the protagonist's ability to commune with it, as critics have readily perceived and as Laguerre himself explicitly explains when Juan Antonio confesses that "sometimes my spirit enters the landscape and molds itself to its perspectives, communing intimately with it" (93), and that "my spirit penetrates everything and it is everything" (143). Sometimes he projects himself into what he observes: "Now it [my spirit] is a flowered liana that entangles itself in the form of an oak" (143); other times he internalizes concrete elements of nature: "The trills of a mockingbird vibrated in me" (36-37); "my soul was filled with morning sun" (83). With exquisite tenderness he uses the diminutive forms *nochecita, mañanita, matita,* and *florecita* ("little night," "morning," "plant," "flower"). Juan Antonio's special sensitivity toward nature suggests associations with the three women in his life. Cold mornings bring memories of Sarah; dusk recalls Delmira; and "everything feminine in Nature seems to have combined in the exhuberant life of Pepiña" (102). He feels he loves each in a different way just as he loves the different moments of nature.

Juan Antonio's perception of nature is not only spiritual, but experienced through the senses as aromas, sounds, colors, and sensations of heat, cold, and dampness. He describes scenes of many colors, but the predominant one is blue. "In the distance the blue ribbon of the sea became confused with the indigo blue sky. . . . Toward the south the sierra raised its blue peaks" (170). Surrounded by the blue of the sea, the mountains and the sky, the circumscribed world of the cane fields seems like an island in itself—perhaps a microcosm of the island of Puerto Rico! One of the most frequent attitudes assumed by the protagonist is trying to see distances, as if wanting to escape from the "insularism" about which Antonio Pedreira wrote, to feel that he is in a more spacious world, as Juan Antonio confides to Pepiña. He seems to continually seek a lookout point from which to extend his vision. Appropriately and symbolically at the end of the novel he reaches his mountain home named Atalaya or Watchtower.

Juan Antonio is an attentive observer of Puerto Rican flora and fauna, and he introduces us to a plethora of local flowers and plants, palm trees, the red flamboyán tree, búcar, moca, guamá, etc., and animal life: the sparrow, peacock, ox, and Puerto Rico's tiny tree frog, the coquí.

In Pedreira's aforementioned prologue to the second edition of *The Blaze* he considers nature the real protagonist of the novel. It does play a major role but, as we have seen, not always in opposition to man, nor does it dwarf the human roles. Nature as viewed in the novel is multifaceted, and, like man, is not always kind. Like Juan Antonio, it has its *"ratitos malos"* ("bad moments") which explode as in the devastating hurricane, obviously that of San Felipe, of 1928. The part of nature which is seen as the enemy is the incursion of sugar cane, whose history is traced:

> On contemplating the splendid cane fields of Los Pozos, I think the cane invades all the fields. It takes possession of a land to which it is not native. And from what remote ages it made itself known! The Chinese used it centuries and centuries ago. It was brought to Europe in the third century, cultivated in Cyprus, Sicily, Madeira, from where it was transported to Santo Domingo. It took to the climate and extended itself throughout tropical America. Everything was propitious and the intruder felt perhaps more than at home. It conquered our plains. Already it climbs the hills and fills the countrysides with its noise of approaching squall. The advent of great milling machinery gave it preponderance. It was the accomplice of the invasion initiated inland, assured the tents of the conquerers. (94)

Cane, then, is an element of nature introduced by man (civilization) and taking over as uncontrollable intruder. In contrast to the jungle which in *The Whirlpool* by José Eustasio Rivera permits nature to devour man, cane has been cultivated as a trap for the poor worker. The transposition of terms which makes civilization the devouring force is underlined by an allusion to Rivera's novel: "Primitivism is being abandoned and one falls in the whirlpool of civilization. Only the color of the skin remains and with time that also will capitulate. The whirlpool of civilization devours it slowly" (211). In this sense too the cane may be an open symbol of all that is foreign to Puerto Rico and does not contribute to its spiritual development or well being, for as Juan Antonio tells us, the jíbaro who loves his parcel of land hates the land that produces cane.

Sugar cultivation as a literary theme in the Caribbean appears less often than coffee and usually with negative connotations. An early Puerto Rican *décima* (ten-line stanza) about the jíbaro's trek to the sugar mill in the early morning cold is full of melancholy and sadness.[9] The Cuban poet Agustín Acosta published in 1926 a long poem entitled *Zafra* [Sugar Making], a lyrical evocation which at the same time expresses social concerns and involves violence, catastrophe, and rebellion. It is likely that Laguerre was familiar with a famous poem by the author of *Puerto Rican Legends and Traditions,* Cayetano Coll y Toste, "El incendio" [The Fire, 1926], which decries the "infamous hand that seeks vengeance" by setting fire to the sugar cane, and admires the generous valor of the former slaves who forgetting the whip help fight the fire.[10] The potential for elaborating such incidents together with the negative aspects associated with sugar cane in literature were there, but it remained for Enrique Laguerre to develop the theme into a first-rate novel. Subsequently it would be treated by the Dominican novelist Ramón Marrero Aristy in *Over* (1939) and by the Puerto Rican author Julio Soto Ramos as recently as 1955, pointing out the ills of absentee ownership, hunger, and misery in his poem "Zafra," perhaps inspired as much by *The Blaze* as by the continued reality of these problems.[11]

Metaphor and Symbol

In this first novel Laguerre shows his mastery of metaphor and symbolism, which will be a constant in his fiction. As Concha Meléndez comments, "he knows that metaphor and symbol are not mere ornaments in the novel but means of clarifying and constructing in large measure the personality of the characters."[12] The use of these artistic techniques may reflect the idea expressed in *The Blaze* of "what is ours," for the jíbaro, like the Argentine gaucho, shows an innate ability to use proverbs and metaphors, as when Chelores asks, "Where will the ox go who doesn't plow?" (53), referring to the worker who no longer works. Juan Antonio listens to his proverbs with delight. Laguerre's use of symbolism is also appealing to the general reader for whom he spells out some meanings quite explicitly, but there are also more subtle metaphors for the more sophisticated reader. Some metaphors are situational while others are stylistic and poetic.

The principal symbol which is situational is the blaze, from which is derived a constellation of metaphors related to fire. Its representation as "the blaze of hatred" is constantly underscored in the novel, but it is at the same time "the circle of fire" of the sun that creates a veritable inferno in the cane fields, the fever which torments the stricken protagonist, the metaphoric fire he uses to "burn his ships behind him," and the real blaze set by the disgruntled peons. These representations as well as the vision of Don Polo's paralysis as a symbol of helplessness against the system give the impression of being derived a posteriori. Laguerre's symbolism never seems artificial, contrived, or strained because it is so intimately rooted in reality and so naturally consequential.

Somewhat more subtle is another elemental symbol, water, which in the novel seems unable to defeat the varied constellation of fire. The misfortunes of the Ventura Rondón family are described as "a deaf river of all adversities, with their ideals sunk in the filthy, stagnant water" (82). Pondering the circumstances which prevented Segundo Marte from realizing his potentials, Juan Antonio notes that "after all, the same thing happens to many of us: we strangle aspirations. We have to drown precious ideals in filthy, stagnant water" (94). On the other hand, Don Polo's conversation, says Juan Antonio, "bubbles in my interior like a fountain of fresh water" (87), but it is not enough to stop the fires of hatred.

If the title is openly symbolical, it is not surprising to find that likewise the subtitles of the divisions of the novel lend themselves to metaphorical interpretation describing at the same time the vicissitudes of cane cultivation and of the protagonist. The "Open Furrows" that receive the seeds in the first chapter parallel the opening of Juan Antonio's experience to "real life" agriculture, not quite what he had bargained for in his studies of agronomy. He is receptive to the new experiences and the implanting of the seeds of future problems and ideals with Segundo's joining the peons and with Don Polo's Socialist ideas. In the second chapter, "While the Cane Grows," Juan Antonio grows also in his knowledge of the people and problems around him. The chapter entitled "Bad Weed" shows Juan Antonio becoming as bad as the cane which enslaves the workers, collaborating openly with the exploiters, and with "Fire," the fourth chapter, the blaze of hatred consumes him as well as the cane. "The Return" is the only title referring exclusively to the protagonist who separates himself definitively from the sugar cane, which, as we have noted previously, suggests symbolism of all that is foreign to the spirit and traditions of the Puerto Rican.

One of the most subtle situational metaphors of the novel is the leitmotif of the conquistador, initiated in the very first words of the book, "I tried to 'burn my ships behind me,'" alluding to Hernán Cortés's stratagem to prevent his crew from retreating. Cortés is explicitly mentioned in this context later in the novel. When first touring the cane fields, Juan Antonio compares himself to a Hispanic conquistador satisfied with his triumphs and with the land he has been granted. He characterizes the experience as Don Quijote's first departure from his home to a world of adventures, imagines Don Flor as Sancho, and in moments of hostility toward Don Polo, "the will and the conscience of men" (203), likens the old man confined to his wheel chair to ridiculous Don Quijote mounted upon Clavileño, a wooden horse, and dubs him "Don Cándido de la Palma Chica" [Don Candid of the Small Palm]. Juan Antonio's retreat to the mountains determined to launch a future "Reconquest" recalls the Spanish Christians' seven-century war of Reconquest that began in the mountainous northern provinces of Spain and was ultimately successful in routing the Moors and in consolidating Spain into a national entity.

Other metaphors provide graphical and lyrical visions akin to those most often found in poetry. Nature, of course, is the most frequent source of metaphor. Chelores the centenarian is seen as "a human cedar" (41); a palm tree as "flirting with a flamboyán tree" (40), and Juan Antonio as "growing dreams in the wheat fields of the future" (25). Other metaphors remind us of the avant-garde imagery of much of the poetry of the time: "My interior movie continues to project the ribbon of memories on the canvas of time" (103); "the train stabbed the night with its headlight" (25). Related to the central image of the title, the Red Socialist banner *"flameó"* (which means both "flamed" and "fluttered") and "floated over the green of the landscape like a tremulous wound" (128).

Psychological Interest

We have observed that *The Blaze,* according to the general formula provided by Fernando Alegría, counterbalances the importance of landscape by accentuating the human factor and by deepening the psychological element. Much of what happens in the novel is dependent upon human defects—megalomania, opportunism, egotism, and vanity—which move Don Oscar, Don Flor, and at times Juan Antonio. The diary initiated in the second chapter is an expression of conscience stirred by the Ventura Rondón incident. The protagonist's struggle between sentiment and reason in a romantic context opens the novel and continues in a social context, leading to hallucinations and nightmares. The resolution of the struggle is not definitive or all-encompassing, for while sentiment and humane feelings finally preside over reason with regard to the social conflict, on the other hand, Juan Antonio's choice of Pepiña over Delmira is in great measure prompted by the rational decision to take a robust wife to ensure healthy offspring, similar to Andrés Hurtado's ideas (inspired by Nietzsche) in Pío Baroja's novel *El árbol de la ciencia* [The Tree of Life], published in Spain in 1911.

It is interesting to note how the first-person narrative affects the psychological portrait of Juan Antonio. It limits our perception to that information he wishes to give us, but he is a flawed narrator in that he is capable of seeing some of his shortcomings, while the reader can see more. Juan Antonio's explanations of his own character are derived from closeness to events, which he observes retrospectively (first chapter) or very close upon their occurrence (beginning with the second chapter). Both *Don Segundo Sombra* and *The Whirlpool* involve first-person memoirs, but in *The Blaze* the point of view seems more closely related to the desire to let the reader delve into the protagonist's motives, something Laguerre would later develop using interior monologue. Juan Antonio's questions regarding social inequities go beyond a psychological conflict in that they lead to existential concerns of man's destiny on earth as a prelude to the return which he completes in the final chapter.

Narrative Structure

The Blaze does not follow what might be called a longitudinal linear structure since the experiences of Juan Antonio in the cane fields are split laterally into five major time frames corresponding to the divisions of the book. In each transversal view Juan Antonio appears, as well as most of the other characters with whom he is involved. This is a structure much more difficult to maintain than a linear approach since each character—and the cast is extensive—reappearing in a new time frame must conserve continuity from the previous delineation. The only slight inconsistency we have noted is in the characterization of Balbino Soltrén, who in the first section seens insensitive but later appears in open sympathy with the peons. This may be in part because we are not witnesses to his change as we are to Juan Antonio's thought processes. The latter provide a nucleus for our interest, but *The Blaze* is as much a novel about the world about him as it is of his own growth.

There is also a sort of circular structure in the novel in that the protagonist first appears renouncing a sentimental past that threatened his professional development and again at the end he renounces another part of his past, this time a rationalistic attitude that threatened his spirit.

Changes of scene within the time frames are effected by asterisks, becoming almost impressionistic once the diary begins in the second chapter. Dramatic tension is sustained by numerous questions posed by the protagonist: "Was I becoming a Socialist?" (77), "Are we to have another 'siege of the foremen'?" (77), "Was I really dominated by that terrible hatred?" (195). Besides the harmonious use of metaphor which we have already noted, what impresses the reader about the clear and graphic prose of Laguerre is the immensely rich vocabulary of flora, fauna, and sugar cultivation which has no corresponding terms in English. Words like *ingenio, trapiche,* and *central* can only be rendered by one word, mill, in English; the nuances of these terms are for those who work daily with them. Nevertheless, Laguerre succeeds in reaching out to all readers, to make them, if they are not natives, at least "transitory" Puerto Ricans.

Chapter Three
Apotheosis of the Jíbaro: *Montoya Plantation*

Laguerre's second novel, *Solar Montoya* [Montoya Plantation], published in 1941, was received with great enthusiasm. Concha Meléndez compared it to the Argentine writer Ricardo Güiraldes's already famous novel of 1926, *Don Segundo Sombra,* in which a boy grows into manhood trying to emulate the ideal gaucho, Don Segundo, who more than a man is an idea and a legend.[1] Laguerre's initial adherence to an illustrious established model, however, should not be taken to reflect any lack of imagination on his part but rather as a thoughtful literary allusion to a tradition similar to the one he is attempting to cultivate. Concha Meléndez observes that the novel has a synthesizing character which combines all the history of Puerto Rico, that of the Indian, the Spaniard, the turbulent era of the seditious parties, and the American takeover.[2] This blending goes even further than historical synthesis, for in *Montoya Plantation* we have literary synthesis, the culmination of the jíbaro genre in Puerto Rico, just as *Don Segundo Sombra* represents the culmination of the gauchesque genre in its time. In Laguerre's novel we see the apotheosis of the mountain jíbaro of the Puerto Rican countryside and the creative synthesis of the various stages of the literary treatment of the jíbaro during approximately a century.

In this respect it is useful to consult the essays on the jíbaro in literature which appear in the anthology *El jíbaro de Puerto Rico; símbolo y figura,* prepared jointly by Enrique Laguerre and Esther M. Melón, and published in 1968. The introductory essay written by Laguerre reviews the stages which have marked the literary treatment of the jíbaro, citing picturesqueness and social focus, associated with what Antonio S. Pedreira calls the first jíbaro cycle, and the poetical creation, represented a good way of life for the jíbaro. Excessive taxation further burdened the coffee plantation owners, whose failure brought with it unemployment and poverty for owner and worker alike. While it must be conceded that government was not responsible for the relentless acts of nature in the form of droughts, floods, and hurricanes which exacerbated the plight of the mountain dwellers, attempts at rehabilitation did not address themselves to the heart of the problem nor did they go beyond feeble programs never effectively implemented. Gonzalo, for example, feels useless as an agent of the Rehabilitation Program, for although he is well meaning, he is simply not prepared to do the job. Other possible relief measures are bogged down in political interests. A young social worker takes cognizance of the fact that in individual cases sometimes extraordinary progress is achieved, but on the whole it is depressing to see how little is done for the many people in need of help. The days of prosperity in the mountain are as legendary as the stories about bandits of old: "Once upon a time coffee was like gold" (422), goes the ironic tale. It is also tremendously ironic that the distressing poverty which afflicts the coffee zone could be alleviated so easily, not by elaborate social programs or handouts, but simply by encouraging restoration of a once thriving industry to its former condition.

Laguerre is not a Naturalist like Zeno Gandía, so he is not at all committed to a fatalistic attitude toward a bad situation, but rather postulates concrete recommendations within the context of his fictional characters and their all-too-real situation. Gonzalo's interest in learning modern methods of farming from his agronomist cousin Juan Antonio Borrás to achieve increased coffee production on less land, a necessity in view of the overpopulation of the island, constitutes an implicit recommendation. Other suggestions are expounded more overtly:

In order to perpetuate mountain living what was needed was love for the land; to unite in common action; to move the will of others; to interest executive leaders of the island; to impede the purchase of coffee plantations from being carried out by third parties; to undertake reforestation; to begin new crops and industries; to recover what has been lost; to resist, resist. . . . Postponing this could well mean suicide. (451–52)

The author, however, does not pretend to have all the answers, for some problems are noted but no solution advanced, leaving a note of

Poetical Creation

The Generation of the 1930s' interest in the jíbaro theme as art sparked the phase of poetic stylization which consciously elevates popular expression to literary awareness with lyricism, symbolism, and other modes of aesthetic elaboration. Laguerre's novel may also be considered poetry in the deepest sense of the word. It is in this category of poetical creation that the author's particular contribution to the jíbaro genre lies, in the artistic skill in blending and in going beyond all the previously mentioned stages into the unique poetic creation that is *Montoya Plantation*.

The very structure of the novel contrasts with the constant spiritual stability of "Compai Lonso." The first half is ascendant in that it follows Gonzalo Mora's growth and development in the shadow of Don Alonso, reflecting the stages associated with the first jíbaro cycle; descriptions of customs and social observation. The fourth of a total of eight chapters leads to Gonzalo's fleeing to New York, the "semideath" from which he awakens in the fifth chapter and begins to learn about the problems which beset the coffee growers. The rest of the novel continues with a descent in the fortunes of Don Alonso and other principal characters observed by Gonzalo after his return. Now the social-protest characteristic of the second jíbaro cycle is dominant, with poetical elaboration of the spiritual legacy of Don Alonso. The closing scene, a quiet dialogue between Gonzalo and a companion of former days, provides a sort of epilogue which completes the final identification of the apprentice jíbaro with his great model. In *Don Segundo Sombra* the respectful title *Don* Fabio signals the young apprentice's transformation into a rancher rather than a wandering gaucho and the inevitable disappearance of a way of life, but in *Montoya Plantation,* the Don accorded to Gonzalo by his old jíbaro friend marks his promotion in the eyes of others to leader of the Montoya traditions. In this way the image of Don Alonso remains firm throughout the novel irrespective of the vicissitudes of fortune, and even continues its ascendant course.

The title of the novel is very different from all the other Laguerrean titles, which are metaphorical in nature, but is perfectly appropriate, for the name of Don Alonso Montoya becomes synonymous with the land itself, the whole area in which his influence was felt. As in the moment of death he grasps the land, he becomes one with it when his surname baptizes the mountain. In contrast we see the name of the once intimidating Corporal Sotomayor grow smaller with adversity and loss of respect, losing the *mayor* (significantly meaning "greater" or "greatest") to become simply Soto and then the diminutive Sotito.

Time is handled differently in the first half of the novel than in the second. As in primitive painting, each detail is treated with care and if the pace seems very slow it is because life in Peña Clara is an invitation to repose. The unsympathetic observer may not perceive the enchantment Gonzalo learns to find in small things, following the examples of Don Jaime Martorell and Don Alonso. "Don Jaime continued living his intense love for the land, although in appearances he lived a monotonous life" (367), the narrator tells us, and the same is true of the young protagonist: "Such was the life of Gonzalo in Peña Clara. Days, months, years. . . . When one lives intensely, he feels the perfect uselessness of parcelled time; the imprint of the man who has existed from within is never erased" (370).

Laguerre's talent as a story teller is perfectly evident in this second novel, in his expert handling of the techniques of foreshadowing and surprise, which enliven the slow-moving first half. There is something disquieting in Gonzalo's telling Don Alonso that he would wish never to leave Peña Clara, to which his protector replies jovially, "Why do you say that? Of course you are not leaving" (317). We barely suspect that the mysterious beggar carrying a figure of a saint, Sotito, is actually Sotomayor, and we are surprised to find out that María Martorell's handsome suitor turns out to be Rodrigo Montoya. Background information is almost imperceptibly introduced, with retrospective narrative handled as each new character appears.

The pace of the first half of the novel is also retarded by the insertion of stories, legends, and verses. This becomes even more complicated as a story within a story within the larger structure of the novel itself emerges when Don Alonso tells the story of how Sergio Plata saved his life and proceeds to recount a story the latter told him about the villainies of the bandit Burgos.

The second half of *Montoya Plantation,* from the fifth to the final chapter, confronts us with an increasingly realistic world in which events move quickly to destroy the way of life represented by Compai

Lonso, while at the same time he seems to move farther away into a more spiritual dimension. The greatest poetic achievement of the novel is without doubt the mythical projection of Don Alonso who embodies the quintessential soul of the mountain dweller to become the metaphysical jíbaro, the soul of Puerto Rico for his young disciple Gonzalo and by extension for the author himself and for the reader. Like the other legendary character in the novel, the bandit Sergio Plata, Don Alonso is portrayed with one foot in the world of palpable, mortal reality and the other in the timeless world of myths.

Laguerre raises the figure of Don Alonso to monumental stature by means of several procedures. He imprints a strong visual emblem in the view of the great jíbaro as a stone centinel high above the valley, with the magnetism of Ubec Peak. The power of Don Alonso's marvelous voice, which "grew in the valley and it seemed that the mountains were speaking" (285) and which "grew in resonances in the depth of the valley" (415), leaves us with an impressive acoustical echo. The image of the jíbaro protagonist also gains in stature by comparison with other coffee growers, with the well-meaning Don Jaime Martorell, who is unable to retain his land, and with the opportunist Don Manuel Ocaña and the irresponsible Don Pedro Ocaña. He also contrasts with the jíbaro workers, with all their varied strengths and weaknesses. Don Alonso surpasses all because he embodies the metaphysical jíbaro. His virtues of strength of will, generosity, persuasion, and tenderness with people, animals, and plants make him "the great jíbaro" (343) and his way of life is a sort of religious experience, that of *"montoyismo"* (362) followed by Gonzalo Mora, a *"montoyero"* (343). His wife, likewise dedicated to love, hospitality, and service to others, is worthy of such a man and the House of Montoya is a refuge for all.

Montoya Plantation, with its many allusions to myths and legends, proves that although legends are often made by history, they may also be made by novelists. The opening sentences prepare us for the birth of a myth by situating us in an atmosphere of timelessness flowing into the moment of historic time which begins the novel:

For centuries life has been rushing forth here. These fountains nurtured the ancient inhabitants. They were born and multiplied until the words brought them to God and the swords to death. . . .

Apotheosis of the Jíbaro: Montoya Plantation

... These first children of the land perished, conquered by the iron of the conquest; but their temples remain. ... Years, centuries passed. And the gallop of thunders: 1898. (243)

The principal means of mythification used in the novel is biblical tone and allusion, appropriate to Don Alonso Montoya's pious devotion to the land and nature. He is called a "patriarch" (445) and a "saint" (452), and like the prophets of old, he passes his labors on to his successor, saying to Gonzalo, "You will be like me" (446). There is a version of the Old Testament episode in which Abraham offers warm hospitality to three strangers who are really messengers of God: Don Alonso is visited by three strangers, health workers who come to administer purgatives to the people to combat the parasite of anemia. Like the biblical patriarch, he welcomes the weary strangers and offers the best of his household to them. The services of Don Alonso and Doña Ana are described in terms suggestive of the Psalms: "It is as if they were shades for hardships, fruit for the hungry, fountains for the thirsty" (304). Don Alonso's fortitude in the face of adversities—the loss of his wife and son Rodrigo, the calamities of nature which afflict the land, the negative attitude of a son and grandson toward the land—raises him to the stature of a suffering Job who will never renounce his faith. His disciple Gonzalo recalls Solomon as he muses, "the benefit of the land is for all: we are all reliant upon the land" (449) and he imagines himself speaking to his beloved with images of nature reminiscent of the Song of Songs (451). At the end of the novel he accepts willingly the call of an immortal conscience he hears and murmurs, repeating Don Alonso's affirmation in the land, and Moses' response before the call of the Eternal, "Here am I" (456).

New Testament allusions are also present. "At times it appeared to Gonzalo that Compai Lonso would lose patience; he lamented that he had been abandoned" (449). Gonzalo's return to Peña Clara suggests that of the prodigal son, with the envy of Don Alonso's other son also hinting at that biblical episode. Finally, Don Alonso's falling to the ground, his arms in the form of a cross, in the presence of his disciple may be considered a allusion to the highest example of sacrifice in the Christian tradition. By chapter 7 several characters are becoming aware of the immortal dimension of the Old Man. The narrator assures us that "alongside Mora, Don Alonso was almost a legend, something that would not die" (431). Gonzalo comments, "You know what I am thinking, Compai Lonso? That to you the years cannot do anything," and the narrator adds that "in truth, Don Alonso was something immaterial" (431). On another occasion Gonzalo tells his tutor, "You do not die," and the narrator explains, "That is to say, the passion of Compai Lonso will never die and the world only exists through passion. Living intensely had created a legend around his life. Jupiter of jíbaro affection, he had his Olympus on the mountain top, the home of a mythical god was his Puerto Rican house" (444). The allusions, as we have seen, extend even beyond the Christian world into that of ancient Greek mythology.

The use of universal and biblical myth has yet another function in addition to that of elevating the figure of Don Alonso, and that is to endow him with universality, providing references in whose contexts the non–Puerto Rican reader as well as the native can perceive the grandeur of this great jíbaro. It becomes the magical poetic ingredient which lends cohesion to local and universal aspects which may be comprehended by all readers.

A Seedbed

A final consideration in our analysis finds that *Montoya Plantation* contains the seeds of many of Laguerre's then future novels. This is most appropriate in view of its theme, the cultivation of the land and the ideal of a productive life in proximity to the soil. A number of later subjects of interest are foreshadowed, some very briefly, but it is clear that they are already present in the author's mind waiting to be developed further. In Gonzalo's childhood there is the sensation of feeling victimized by adults which in *The Fingers of the Hand* will determine in large measure the protagonist's attitude toward society. His flight to New York, treated very schematically, is a preview of the theme of emigration treated later in *The Ceiba Tree in the Flower Pot* and in *The Labyrinth*. At the same time concern with social and moral implications of changes occurring on the island, already notable in *The Blaze,* is reaffirmed and firmly established as an integral part of Laguerre's fiction. Indignation is expressed against Latin American tyrants when Gonzalo sees a photograph of a bemedalled general in the newspaper; this will later be developed in *The Labyrinth* and *Fire and Its Air*. In spite of having been brought up under Don Alonso's tutorship, Gonzalo experiences moments of doubt, fragmentation, and confused identity like so many of Laguerre's future protagonists, and on contemplating the uselessness of his job with Rehabilitation, he fears he is betraying his generation (445) in the same way that Víctor Sandeau does in *River Bed without a River*. The novel also offers a bipartite structure which is repeated in *River Bed* and in *Benevolent Masters*.

In addition to thematic seeds, we can also trace some of Laguerre's novelistic procedures to *Montoya Plantation,* particularly the use of legend, myth, or fable which marks all subsequent novels in some form or another, symbolic value accorded to or deduced from certain episodes (as when Don Alonso liberates a dog which has been tied up), and repetition of lyrical leitmotifs. The technique of interior monologue is used sparingly in italics, something Laguerre later develops as a major technique. Another interesting aspect of his fiction which makes its appearance here is the intermixing of fictional "reality" with that of the outside world when Gonzalo's reading of Juan Antonio Borrás's copy of *The Blaze* (Laguerre's book, of course) inspires his return to Don Alonso's house. This reminds us of what occurs in the second part of the *Quijote* when the fictional characters discuss the first part and the fame of Don Quijote. Already established, too, is Laguerre's tendency to form one novelistic world inhabited by characters who reappear from the pages of other novels to give us the impression that his fictional world is dear to him and former children of his literary creation are not forgotten.

Chapter Four
Two Solitary Lives

El 30 de febrero [The 30th of February], of 1943, and *Los dedos de la mano* [The Fingers of the Hand], of 1951, Laguerre's third and fifth novels, involve protagonists who are afflicted by great solitude. Although the introverted hunchback Teófilo Sampedro of *The 30th of February* is very different from the attractive, ambitious social climber Lucha Madrigal of *The Fingers of the Hand,* both are essentially misfits who are dissatisfied with their lot and become obsessed by their respective handicaps, physical in the one, social in the other. They live at odds with themselves, Teófilo fleeing from his deformed shadow, Lucha from her "other self." Both experience a difficult childhood, which partially explains why they do not reach out to others with affection. Their silences are disconcerting to those who care for them; unable to communicate with others, they fail to appreciate problems which do not involve them personally and consume themselves in resentment. A sense of inferiority expresses itself in different ways but each is very alone. In both novels, too, fables and fairy tales are related to the protagonists' experience and the principal characters move in very real social settings in which serious problems exist. Despite the differences between the two novels with regard to narrative style, setting, and general content, they are basically stories about characters who experience tremendous loneliness and lead sterile lives.

The 30th of February

In the forward Alonso Guilarte explains that he has reconstructed in biographical form the diary of a university schoolmate, Teófilo Sampedro, left in his hands by the young man's mother, Doña Eusebia. Refraining from judgment, he presents the "incomprehensible" life of Sampedro in "five episodes." In the first, entitled "Asylum," the twenty-one-year-old Teófilo, who has lived in Puerta de Tierra since the age of six, recalls vague impressions of early childhood in a small town of the interior. He is teased by other children because of his hunched back, but goes along with the forays of the neighborhood gang and despite the difficult life of poverty in the swampy El Mangle ("Mangrove") slum, where he lives with his mother, he finds some measure of solace in his friendship with the old black fisherman Andrade, who tells him stories of pirates and the sea. Eusebia, beset by poverty and illness, is able to place her son in an asylum where he can study, thanks to Don Ángel Santos, "zealous guardian of public morality" and well-known benefactor of poor children. He suffers ridicule, loneliness, and repression, eventually adapts, and finishes his secondary studies, seeking refuge in dreams and tales and ever dreaming of flight from the institution and from himself—his deformed shadow, which is his worst enemy. Teófilo hears of old Andrade's death and is stricken with what is diagnosed as heart trouble. Upon leaving the asylum he catches sight of a card in the director's office that states, "Father: Unknown," but his mother later assures him it is an error.

The episode entitled "First Boarding House" sees Sampedro attending the University of Puerto Rico to fulfill his mother's dream. Don Ángel Santos and another gentleman are financing his first semester and his mother works hard despite ill health to help him. She informs him that the error on his card from the asylum has been corrected to show that his father is José Sampedro. A professor cruelly discourages Teófilo from enrolling in teaching because of his defect, so he registers in secretarial studies. He lives in the boarding house of Doña Paquita, who supports her frivolous daughters and useless son. Sampedro quietly accepts a new nickname (he never seems to be able to escape these nicknames), Doctor Faustus, and is obliged in freshman hazing to act out the part with Margarita Santos, daughter of Don Ángel. Because of a student strike and loss of clients, Doña Paquita is forced to close her house and move away with her daughters, one of whom—Hortensia—is the object of Teófilo's secret love.

In "Second Boarding House" Teófilo is taken in by the charitable Doña Suncha and continues to suffer occasional allusions to his handicap, observing the student atmosphere, the formation of a cultural group, and the superficial conversations of the young people who seem unable to take anything seriously, including their studies. Teófilo's sense of alienation increases, but he finds tolerance and cordiality in his roomate Germán, nicknamed "Peripherical," and in a rather unhappy black girl named Camila. In a conversation Germán speaks cynically of Teófilo's aspirations being realized "the 30th of February."

In "Fable," Teófilo wins the fable contest sponsored by the newly founded student newspaper of that title and momentarily comes out of his shell. He evades another hunchbacked student who is not at all insecure in spite of his defect. Teófilo hears that Hortensia has gone mad and discovers that Teté, a student he had thought frivolous, has another side that she calls her "interior kingdom." He overhears Doña Suncha's conversation with another woman about him in which it is mentioned that José Sampedro is not his father but his uncle. Distraught, he returns home, and becomes ill and delirious.

In the final episode, ". . . And a 9th of May Came," Doña Eusebia at her son's bedside recalls how she had been deceived by a more mature, educated man who was a guest in the home of her uncle, who had brought her up and who later adopted her child. She also recalls Teófilo's fall down a staircase which deformed his back. When the latter recovers from his delirium, mother and son affectionately promise each other to clarify the circumstances of his birth after he graduates, during summer vacation. Embarrassed to return to Doña Suncha's, Teófilo commutes from Puerta de Tierra until a new transfer student, Manuel, offers his aunt Julia's hospitality. He is accepted gladly by Doña Julia, who also offers her home to Don Ángel's daughters—Margarita and Ester Santos—and another girl. Teófilo enjoys speaking to Margarita and feels at ease with her, but Ester is inexplicably hostile. Manuel notes that there is "something in the physiognomy of Teófilo that reminds me of Ester" (670).[1] Meanwhile Ester has heard that Teófilo is her half-brother but refuses to believe it. We are informed rather abruptly of Teófilo's death. Margarita accepts the fact that Teófilo was her brother and the students, in whose campus life the hunchbacked young man only participated marginally, pay their sincere respects to the grieving mother.

The theme of the hunchback of course harkens back to the famous *Hunchback of Notre Dame* (1833) by Victor Hugo, one fable which surprisingly Teófilo never mentions. It is always interesting to see how different authors manage similar themes, and curiously enough, we find that another novelist born the same year as Laguerre, Francisco Ayala, published in Spain in 1926 his first novel, *Tragicomedia de un hombre sin espíritu* [Tragicomedy of a Man without a Spirit], which was about a hunchbacked youth. In both Ayala's and Laguerre's novels a manuscript written by the protagonist is found in Cervantine fashion but the narrative is rendered in the third person, there is both humor and sadness, the protagonists seek refuge in books, identifying themselves with fiction, and respond to their deformities in similar ways. Ayala's *Tragicomedy* is the story of Miguel Castillejo, whose solitary youth as the butt of jokes makes him cultivate pessimism, cynicism, and indifference. The contrasts between the two novels, however, are equally impressive, for while Teófilo Sampedro is driven by his own shadow to defeat, Miguel Castillejo acts to take revenge but discovers in the process that some people without physical defects can be more ridiculous than he and that it is healthier to laugh than to despair.

The 30th of February is a multi-faceted novel and perhaps for this reason has not been fully appreciated by the critics, who find its principal merit as a psychological novel.[2] It is similar to *The Blaze* in that the protagonist's psychological problems are developed alongside the depiction of the world about him, although Teófilo's inner anxieties seem more justified because of the tremendous problems his handicap creates. In view of the previous novels of Laguerre, it was to be expected that *The 30th of February* would largely rest upon the pillars of the protagonist's psychology and the social ambience. There is, however, another dimension to the novel hinted at in *The Blaze* when Juan Antonio Borrás's experiences eventually lead him to ultimate questions about man's destiny on earth, and that is the philosophical dimension. *The 30th of February* has definite existential projections which have not been duly appreciated. The protagonist himself alludes to the three major dimensions of the novel when he asks: "Was it an exclusive illness or that of a whole generation? Or perhaps of all humanity?" (537), inquiring in effect whether the problem of insecurity and indefensiveness is personal, social, or universal.

With regard to the psychological element, Concha Meléndez states that "Sampedro, the protagonist, is a psychological study in which the author traces the effects of the physical deformity of the character and his spiritual misfortune" in addition to being observer of a generation in crisis; Zayas Micheli sees in Sampedro the first great Laguerrean characterization and carries out an extensive psychological analysis of the protagonist's attempt to adapt his spirit to his circumstance.[3] According to Zayas, Teófilo faces a triple dilemma, confronting the world of the healthy who repel the handicapped, his own destiny of an afflicted man who must integrate his illness to his life and accept it, and the slum and student atmospheres in which he moves. The critic, referring to Karl Jaspers, describes Teófilo's "psychopathic" condition aggravated by the attitude of his mother in keeping the secret of his birth. Feeling himself too visible and the object of ridicule, he leads a "frontier existence" between reality and fantasy, seeking to evade himself. Defenseless and unable to integrate successfully, he grows in his sentimental life, with feelings of resentment, envy, and dissatisfaction. In his quite complete and detailed analysis Zayas cites the importance of the dream in which Teófilo sees himself without the deformity and of his desire to avoid "the other," another hunchbacked student who manages to cope successfully with his handicap. Zayas sees Teófilo's prize-winning fable of the little lamb whose life is endangered in the forest while two owls discuss whether he should remain standing or seated as a reflection of the fracture between the protagonist and the world around him. This may be so, but actually the fable is an allusion to a debate in Puerto Rico about whether the lamb in the official coat of arms should be standing up or lying down, while the problem of Puerto Rico's destiny was being ignored. Significantly the lamb asks, "What good is it to discuss whether I should be seated or standing if I am always at the mercy of the lion or the eagle?" (614). He is referring, of course, to the lion of Spain's coat of arms and to the eagle representing the United States.

The social dimensions of the novel involve the portrayal of several types of societies through which the protagonist passes. The first is the undisciplined gang of slum hoodlums, the next is the controlled and regimented society of the asylum which nurtures the children's cruelty and suffocates the protagonist's spirit, and then the unconcerned society of the university students dedicated to frivolity and indifferent to the responsibilites of adulthood. The university mob chooses very appropriate names for their ventures as *Nadaístas* ("Nothing-ists"), their amateur theater—*Farsa* ("Farce"), and their newspaper—*Fábula* ("Fable"), characterizing their retreat into nothing, farce, and childhood fable. Their Mutual Admiration Society is a reflection of the adult world with its unabashed hypocrisy and hyperbole in which the prominent symbol of morality, Don Ángel Santos, is neither angel nor saint, and in which mediocrity is celebrated as genius. Yet all is not denunciation, for the reader is impressed with the large number of really charitable people, those who practice "charity without nails," like Teófilo's friend from the asylum, Roberto, his sacrificing mother, Doña Eusebia, the loving old black fisherman Andrade, the generous Doña Suncha, the sensitive Carmen, the unselfish Doña Julia, and the understanding Margarita Santos, but Teófilo's radical solitude prevents him from coming out of his self-imposed shell and appreciating fully the goodness in many of the people around him.

The novel presents a graphic picture of various places in the San Juan and Río Piedras areas. We see life in El Mangle, a slum of mud and grinding poverty, a path which leads its youth to jail or the hospital, but where a helpful old fisherman and the young troublemakers are capable of helping a sick mother by putting up a shack on the muddy shore. We see the contrasts between the haves and the have nots in grim reality and in jest, when not far from the misery of the slums a sumptuous carnival parade up Ponce de León Avenue spurs an observer to imagine what would happen if everything those people had not yet paid for disappeared. There are descriptions of the old part of San Juan in which "the glory of a people of great traditions" is eternalized (510), in contrast to the noisy commercial districts. Laguerre recreates university life in Río Piedras, freshmen hazing, the boarding houses, transformations which occur in the students who come there from the island, and the character of the university town. This is largely achieved by the extensive reproduction of conversations among the students which make us feel immersed in their world.

In view of the fact that much existential literature concerns the difficulties of the individual in society, it is not difficult to see how closely related are the social and philosophical dimensions of the novel.

Teófilo Sampedro cannot accept the values and mores of those around him and feels continually isolated and alone in a world and even a universe whose purpose he cannot fathom. Like Segismundo in Calderón de la Barca's famous play *La vida es sueño* [Life Is a Dream], he laments his birth, "If I had not been born" (476), and comments that "being is so painful in certain circumstances" (596). His existential anguish is individual; he feels alienated from others, even though people seem to like the sullen youth and when he is ill show their concern for him. His aloneness cannot be eased because it is existential and not just psychological; it goes beyond the social medium because he feels abandoned from infancy and thrown into a hostile universe. This is suggested symbolically by the mystery surrounding his origin and the disappearance of his father after placing him in the world, like that of a God abandoning his creation. Teófilo also experiences what appears to be a symbolical fall from grace when as a child he falls down a staircase, a traumatic incident that haunts his memory and is responsible for the broken back which will be the cross he must bear for the rest of his life. He asks, "Why this responsibility of continuing to live bleeding if he was not guilty of his misfortune?" (529). This anguished question is parodied when one of the upperclassmen acts out a scene supposed to represent Dante's Inferno and asks: "What sin did this soul commit who carries the bundle?," referring to Teófilo's deformity (561). Religious allusions are of great significance, for in the boarding house nicknamed "The Abode of the Blessed," only Teófilo, continually hearing the accusation of being ungrateful, finds no solace in his existence. His mother, on the other hand, relies on her religion and unselfishly says she hopes St. Peter will bless those who are more fortunate, which is ironic in view of the surname (*Sampedro* means "San Pedro" or "Saint Peter") of her family. The name *Teófilo*, meaning "theophile" or "one who loves God," is also ironic in that Teófilo Sampedro finds it difficult to subscribe to his friend Luis Soto's faith. When Teófilo asks him if he believes in God, Soto answers: "Definitely yes. I cannot avoid it, although I do not believe in that God of convenience that others fabricate for their own benefit. Who can feel the influence of the Infinite and not believe in a Force and a Harmony of which one forms part?" (557). Teófilo's reason "proved useless to capture the why of creation" (591). Attending mass with his mother, he notes that "the priests talked of resigning oneself, of submitting to the dictates of Divine Providence, but he already experienced a confusing sensation of finding himself abandoned by God" (645). Teófilo's aforementioned fable thus assumes another dimension, since the lamb is a traditional emblem of Christ; the plight of the lamb suggests Christ's final enigmatic lament that God had forsaken him.

Feeling himself utterly alone in a universe devoid of purpose, Teófilo Sampedro cannot change the biblical Peter's initial denial into faith. He finds his concrete existence something he cannot deny. Carrying his burden, he is unable to find a life project, constantly lamenting that he serves no purpose. He defines himself as an "interim" man, for he is caught between the dark mysteries of an unknown past and those of an impossible future, a thirtieth day of February. Not knowing his origin, he cannot face his destiny. He is circumscribed by darkness, the same darkness of the womb and of death, for he envies the tree, ignorant of its death. "Knowledge hurts at times," he recognizes (508), for which reason the nickname Doctor Faustus seems appropriate. He feels drawn to darkness and to the sea, which, according to Jorge Manrique's famous metaphor, is death.

Teófilo Sampedro, while maintaining his consistency and uniqueness as a concrete protagonist, is at the same time a human being who lives in existential anguish inquiring about his origin and purpose and suffering radical aloneness. Perhaps the protagonist's physical deformity is also an allusion to the famous existentialist philosopher Kierkegaard, who suffered from the same. Additional allusions to the Spanish existentialist Miguel de Unamuno may be seen in the wordplay of *sobrevivir* and *sobremorir* ("surviving" and "sur-dying"), the epigraph of the novel quoting the fictional protagonist, and the protagonist's existence between the real world and that of fantasy akin to that of Augusto Pérez between his life and "mist" in *Niebla* [Mist].

The reiterated references to fairy tales, stories, legends, and fables appear in connection with the three major levels we perceive in the novel: psychological, social, and philosophical. Teófilo retreats from early youth into the world of illusions, dreams, and adventure stories to compensate for his frustration. Society also has its fantasies, as in the public image of Don Ángel Santos and in the display of grandeur in the parade which one observer imagines in disarray if all the items bought on credit were to disappear. One student calls Professor Noriega's book of poems "the emperor's suit," referring to Andersen's famous tale "The Emperor's New Clothes" (based on an earlier story by Juan Manuel), in which the emperor is deluded into believing himself richly dressed in public when he is in fact naked. Pomales adds, "Many are the emperor's clothes that are woven on our island" (599). Another notes that professors, politicians, and poets wear them and Alonso Guilarte, the transcriber of Teófilo's story, concludes that "the greatest suit is worn by the whole island," fashioned by the "fantastic weavers" who speak of a marvelous island for tourism ignoring its poverty. The students themselves seem to prefer a world of fables to the real world, turning everything into light banter and material for fables. And finally, with the closing words of the novel, "The fable ends," life is equated with fable. As one of the students remarks, "We all live fables" (598). Perhaps all of us are interim beings existing between the mystery of origin and an equally obscure 30th of February, although not everyone feels in the burdens of life the existential anguish of Teófilo Sampedro.

The Fingers of the Hand

The novel presents the story of Lucrecia (Lucha) Madrigal and her long-standing animosity toward the aristocrats of her town, Naranjales, represented by the "Torre without *s*" family who distinguish themselves from the plebeian Torres, who have dropped a string of prestigious surnames to become simply "Torres." She is reminded of her own humble origin by the disparaging nickname Lucha Mesón ("Tavern"), alluding to the tavern her mother runs. In spite of the aversion she feels toward the tobacco workers employed in the major industry of the town, her sweetheart is Juan Soler, who not only is one of them but also a Socialist activist, as is his mother, Dolores (niece of Dolorito Montojo of the novel *The Undertow,* who has changed her name, better to serve the cause, and dons men's slacks to go out among the workers to preach social justice.

Lucha is anxious to study at the University of Puerto Rico and to leave her uncomfortable home life marred by her mother's bad humor and authoritarianism and by her uncle's drunken insults. She recalls a traumatic childhood incident when Uncle Pedro, first husband of Aunt

Cruz, broke down the door to get his daughter Camila and injured the defenseless women so that Emma, Lucha's mother, had to use crutches and Lucha herself bears a scar, both physical and emotional. She also recalls the story of her father's miraculous rescue many years before when his boat capsized at sea and he was rescued thanks to a gull who traced circles overhead attracting attention to the foundering fisherman, but later he disappeared at sea, "lost between two solitudes" (378).[4] Discouraged and alienated by Lucha's noncommittal behavior toward him, Juan marries a humble member of the prestigious Torre del Salto family, Adelaida Matías. Lucha sees an advantage of prestige in the teaching profession and upon graduation decides to return to conquer Naranjales from her new position, which gains her entrance into Villa Monserrate, the Torre del Salto family home. She uses the discord that exists between the nieces of Doña Monserrate to her advantage and manages to ingratiate herself with the old lady, attract her nephew Serafín, and gain acceptance in high society, thanks to her wiles and fortune-telling ability. During visits to the Juan Soler family she feels envious at times of the life she might have led and the son that might have been hers, but driven by her blind ambition, Lucha invents some illustrious ancestors and succeeds in marrying Adolfo Cáceres from a family that gained ascendancy over the Torre del Salto family. Returning from a condolence call to Juan, whose wife had died, Lucha meets with the anger of her husband from whom she alienates herself, inviting Juan to be her "vice-husband." She contrives a situation in which Serafín, her collaborator in cultural projects, feels threatened by her jealous husband and kills him.

The political boss and tobacco czar Don Arturo Pasamonte y Velazco (called *Don Puro,* which means "cigar") is elected senator and the new Socialist leader Silvestre Cuartos works with him to form a Patriotic Alliance "in which capital and work are joined" (463). Lucrecia attracts and marries Don Puro but is unable to dominate him as she would like. A crisis in the market leads to deals between the Pasamonte & Wilks Tobacco Co. and the American Tobacco Co., which are prejudicial to the workers, who rebel. Lucha discovers the name of the girl her husband deceived many years ago is Magdalena Solares, who she suspects is Dolores Soler. Tricking Dolores into confessing the truth, that Juan is indeed the illegitimate son of Don Puro, Lucha expects to curtail the Socialist activities of Juan against her husband's firm. Neither father nor son is perturbed by the news, and eventually an agreement between the workers and the company is worked out. Small tobacco producers, betrayed by Don Puro, set fires to the warehouses and seeing bad times ahead, Lucha advises her husband to sell out to his American partner, Wilks, which he refuses to do. Meanwhile, her mother-in-law confides that her son Puro is really the son of a man she loved but did not marry, and not a legitimate, "pure" Pasamonte. Don Puro loses all his capital in bad deals and Lucha leaves him, going with her mother and uncle to live in a beach house in Loíza. She disappears one day in a small rowboat she had named "Gull," which some fishermen find carrying aboard "all the weight of the anguish and solitude of the world" (517).

    The title, as in most of Laguerre's novels, is significant and symbolical, referring principally to Lucha's ability to manage others as if they were the fingers of her hand. She accomplishes this largely by using the hands of others, reading their palms to encourage them to play into her hands by the power of suggestion and compliments. Hands are a recurring motif: the hands of the angry workers raised in protest; hands lowered in discouragement; the fingers of Uncle Pedro working the door open in the terrible childhood incident she remembers; her father's hand injured by a spiny gill of a fish, which prevented him from becoming a doctor; Don Puro's hands burned in a warehouse fire; and her own hand upon which is written the destiny of someone she wants and doesn't want to be. The reiterated allusions in the novel itself may be complemented by a statement in *The 30th of February,* that the number of distinguished families left in Río Piedras can be counted on the fingers of the hand, for it is obvious that in Naranjales also the aristocrats of yesteryear are disappearing, losing their wealth due to weakness, indolence, and bad administration, their vitality consumed in dissension and vanity. Nature also has its fingers—the stems of tender plants which attract Lucha and of tobacco plantings mutilated by the irate workers.

    Lucha's problem is implicit even in her name, meaning "struggle" or "war."[5] As a child she was quarrelsome and early in the novel she tells a suitor, a future minister, that "a lion attracts me more than a lap dog" (340). She lives in perpetual struggle against the backdrop of other wars, those which divide classes, families, and nations (the First World War). She herself is at war with the town of Naranjales in general, the "big people," and herself.

Laguerre makes it quite clear that Uncle Pedro's bestiality, difficulties with her mother and Uncle Emilio, and her father's disappearance have left their mark on Lucha. She feels that men have failed her (an inverse situation exists in Laguerre's later novel *Los amos benévolos* [Benevolent Masters], where women are blamed). Feeling unloved, Lucha is in turn unloving. Nevertheless we are not dealing with a Naturalistic novel in which environment exacts an inexorable price because she seems to invite her own destiny with her "hieratical" nature. Even if other men have failed her, Juan has been an attentive boyfriend and one may well ask why, if her hatred toward her mother and Uncle Emilio is so deep, she misses them while attending college and at the end of the novel goes back to them. Perhaps the unpleasant incidents serve as reasons to justify herself to her own eyes; in the midst of despair Lucha feels like crying "for herself, for what she could have been and wasn't because *everyone fails me and I weary myself trying to keep ahead of them*" (439). She sees herself as a fish about to get trapped and is quick to disclaim responsibility, blaming her problems on the "big people"—including adults and those with power in society, religion, and politics—and even on her ancestors. Surely Lucha's childhood experiences influence her hostility, but we do not think Laguerre accepts them as controlling factors. Lucha's character has a lot to do with how she responds to these experiences.

Lucha's greatest struggle is to reconcile her own contradictions which lead her to ambivalent behavior, as when she tells Juan bluntly, "I don't want to share my life with anyone" (350), only to ask him if he will fill her empty world. In another conversation she confesses to him that "I do things that I myself do not approve of" (383). "Her whole life is reduced to a mad struggle to outflank 'the big people'" (471). Lucha tells Juan that her greatest struggle has been not being able to forget him and he recognizes her problem: "You have lived like another person" (510). She often speaks of living one life alongside another and of "the other" person she is. The schism in her own being which she cannot control as easily as she controls others leads to her eventual defeat and she disappears, like her father, between two solitudes, leaving some doubt as to the possible influence of heredity, of a Naturalistic leaning, or a decision on the part of Lucha to put an end to the war with herself and the world.

Lucha's life is projected against a background of troubled times in Puerto Rico, the Socialist movement's struggle for workers' rights. The local heroes are Juan and Dolores Soler, who follow the leadership of Sandalio Villegas, whose name is strikingly reminiscent of that of Santiago Iglesias (beginning with *Sa--*, ending in *-as*, with the same number of syllables similarly stressed), the founder of the Insular Workers' party in 1908, which later became the Socialist party. In the novel, as in reality, the ideals of the Socialists are corroded by opportunists like Silvestre Cuartos (*cuartos* is slang for "cash"), who collaborates with Don Puro to form the Patriotic Alliance which supposedly unites capitalists and workers, or like Serafín Torre del Salto, who changes his name to Torres in a public display of solidarity with the proletariat but doesn't mind profiteering. While Laguerre's sympathies evidently are with the workers, he seems to suggest that Dolores Soler's Socialist zeal goes too far in suppressing sentimentality. Lucha berates her for preaching social equality while ignoring her own humble family as if they were an inferior caste. We see Dolores correct that situation in the novel and become more humanized. Dolores Soler seems modeled after Luisa Capetillo (1880 or 1882–1922), a Socialist labor organizer, defender of women's and workers' rights, first woman to defiantly wear slacks in public in Puerto Rico, and mother of three children out of wedlock.

The protagonist sees the whole town as her enemy, symbolized best by its two dominant buildings, the church and the tobacco factory: "This town! Stuck like a wedge of sorrows in the raw flesh of the hills . . ." (355). She returns determined "to step on the whole town" (397), to impose herself as Lucrecia Madrigal where she had been called Lucha Mesón. Naranjales itself is torn between the demands of the workers and those of the church, which are for peace and quiet, between the dark hands that are raised in protest and the pale feminine hands that support José el Santero (who makes the images of saints).

Beyond the town other events are taking place, like the World War, which situates part of the novel between 1914 and 1918. Lucha only becomes aware of the war when she is unable to secure Chinese silk for her debut in the Casino and she projects her own motives, saying that wars have only one purpose, to take things away from one another. It seems closer to home when a balladeer friend of Dolores is lost when a ship is sunk between Puerto Rico and New York, which reminds Lucha of her father's disappearance, and when Juan Soler and Serafín Torre del Salto are drafted. On the other hand, the war is a "blessing" for the Pasamonte & Wilks tobacco enterprises. Another international event more directly felt in the novel is the economic crisis of the late 1920s in which Don Puro Pasamonte is caught up and ruined, marking the end of Lucha's ambitions.

The theme of social ambition in a woman had previously been treated by the Venezuelan novelist Rómulo Gallegos in his novel *La trepadora* [The Climber, 1925], as Zayas Micheli notes.[6] It is also present, however, in the well-known novel *La desheredada* [The Disinherited Woman, 1881] by Benito Pérez Galdós, set against historical and political events in Spain. In Galdós's novel the protagonist is obsessed with proving her nobility while falling into the deepest degradation. In *The Fingers of the Hand* Laguerre assumes a narrative tone that is strikingly new, in view of his previous novels, a very present ironic voice that is reminiscent of Galdós. In contrast to other Laguerre novels, the narrator is not a character or transcriber, but rather an omniscient voice which incorporates the point of view of different characters with ironic overtones or arouses the reader's indignation toward certain events by the deliberate use of sarcasm. Sometimes the voice is melodramatic, others festive, and the narrative irony is particularly strong regarding matters of exaggerated religiosity, political deceit, and social hypocrisy.

Speaking of the missionary friend of Lucha's mother, the narrator pretends to admire "such abnegated missionary dedication that she forgot to get a husband and children" (334). He notes that the same women who support José el Santero against the workers' protest have children who are dying of hunger. He assumes the pious Doña Monserrate's perspective in praising her complete dedication to God, for "it is what is expected of all good Christian women" (370), but later views her from the point of view of her nephew, disappointed at not inheriting her estate, as having been in life "nothing more than a mummified specimen of egotism and idiocy" (449). It is very clear that the "Christian example of Aunt Monse," who is deaf and blind to everything happening in her home—or the world, for that matter—because she is too busy praying, is not as admirable as the narrator says.

Irony is rampant in references to the social conflict when the narrator feigns hostility toward Dolores Soler: "The truth, only the truth. Before the manlike woman came, preceding Sandalio Villegas, peace reigned in the town. . . . Before, everyone gave thanks to God because in the town there was a factory; all were grateful to Don Puro Pasamonte and Mr. Stanley Wilks. Everyone" (349). Speaking for the "decent people," he acts indignant at Sandalio Villegas's insinuations that working conditions are unclean and he parodies the town's unequivocal devotion to their benefactor: "Señor [which means both "Mr." and "Lord"] Don Puro Pasamonte! Do not abandon us and deliver us from evil" (350).

Sarcasm is extremely evident when the narrator contemplates hypocrisy. Of Lucha's dedication to her first husband, Adolfo, he assures us that it is difficult to find a woman more dedicated to love" (437) and after Adolfo's death, for which Lucha is largely responsible, she is depicted as a "defenseless widow" who grieves for "her unforgettable Adolfo." The narrator refers to Senator Pasamonte's desire to reinforce the brotherhood between rich and poor, but with "'everyone in his place' like the good Don Puro said" (467). With obvious irony we are informed:

> The day of elections, Adolfo Cáceres, well accompanied by many other dead men, came to vote in favor of the candidacy of Don Arturo Pasamonte y Velazco. The strangest thing is that they voted in full compliance with all the requirements of the law. In addition, no small number of Sandalio Villegas's followers remained without voting because a number of other people wished to do them the favor of voting for them. (458)

Such election frauds were all too common in Puerto Rico.

In some cases the irony is in a less serious vein, as in a reference to the American mother of Lucha's friend Dolly MacDonald, an "amphibian" Puerto Rican who prefers the prestige of her maternal surname: "Mistress MacDonald came to the island to see natives and the natives saw her without having to pay for costly trips" (383). In general the narrative style is flexible, alternating third-person narration with interior monologue recalling past events, slipping from inconspicuous objectivity to blatent sarcasm.

This is one of Laguerre's most ironic novels, filled with ironic contrasts and situations. When Lucha is about to leave for college, the tobacco workers announce that they will sponsor her education—the same workers whose sweat and smell of tobacco irritate her. Ironic also are the two revelations in the novel, that Juan Soler is not of plebeian family but instead the son of Don Puro Pasamonte y Velazco, and that the latter, the supposed scion of aristocratic birth, is really a plebeian. Near the end of the book there is an ironic meeting of two processions crossing as they go through the town, one a funeral cortege for a worker killed in a riot, the other a carnival parade with its representation of a royal coronation. Also ironic is Lucha's final act which imitates her father's adventure, with the "gull" bringing death instead of salvation. There is irony in Lucha's dislike of fairy tales, which she sees as inventions of adults to control children, but she feels like Cinderella at her first ball in the Casino and becomes virtually a fairy tale character in her role as fortune-teller, bringing about her wishes by the art of suggestion.

Perhaps the greatest irony of all is the most difficult to perceive and yet the saddest. Lucha and Juan are essentially fighting the same enemy, the "big people" who take advantage of others, although they work against each other. Juan goes about the task in a constructive way, advocating change and legislative action, while Lucha's course of trying to humiliate the strong by becoming one of them is ultimately self-defeating.

Chapter Five
An Important Period of History

La resaca [The Undertow], published in 1949, represents a departure from the three novels which preceded it and even from Laguerre's subsequent works in that it is longer, probes the protagonist's thoughts less, is panoramic in the geographical scope of the island, reads like an adventure novel in several parts, and treats a period of Puerto Rico's past prior to the author's lifetime. Angelina Morfi called it "the high point of his novelistic art," citing other equally encomiastic response on the part of critics.[1] While we find it difficult to choose one particular novel of Laguerre's as his best, as in the case of the prolific nineteenth-century Spanish novelist Benito Pérez Galdós, we do recognize it as his most ambitious and unique work.

The "Bionovel"

The neologism which appears as the subtitle of *The Undertow*, *"bionovela,"* points to the fact that the life story of Dolorito Montojo forms the novelistic framework which we shall summarize briefly since specific events will be treated with more detail later. The first part, as Morfi notes, provides a symbolical foreshadowing with the young Dolorito's bold defense of a pregnant slave being whipped by an overseer followed by his accidental fall into an abandoned well (representing the general atmosphere of the times) while trying to save a baby bird (Puerto Rico). In contrast the mountain Yukiyú serves as a spiritual sentinel and symbol of the aspirations of the protagonist for freedom.[2] His home environment is characterized by extreme poverty, the irresponsible nature of his father, and the religious anguish of his mother Lina. Also presented is the contrast between the two local landowners, Don Pedro Quiroga, a somewhat mysterious Puerto Rican liberal who lives at *La Mina* ("The Mine"), which had previously belonged to the Montojo family, and Don Nicolás Velazco, Spanish traditionalist who owns Monte Grande. The two live at odds with each other, resulting in ill will between the workers on both lands and the death of an innocent party, Dolorito's uncle.

The second part of the novel follows the schooling of Dolorito by the kindly Don Cristóbal Amorós (called Don Cristo [Christ]), who inspires spiritual elevation and idealism. In contrast, the eccentric bachelor Don Felipe Santoro tutors a poor relative just arrived from Soria, Balbino Pasamonte, in cynicism and ascent to power. The latter learns quickly, ingratiating himself with Don Nicolás Velazco, in whose house he is allowed to live, to the dismay of Don Nicolás's daughter Lucía, who secretly meets with her lover, Lorenzo Quiroga, son of her father's enemy. Lorenzo is mysteriously killed, an innocent peon imprisoned, and Balbino installed as lord of the manor married to Lucía, whose parents leave for Spain. Dolorito's secret love, Rosario, is dishonored by the rural policeman friend of Balbino, Gil Borjes, and disappears accompanied by Dolorito's sister Rosa, who has married his childhood companion Juan Gorrión. At eighteen years of age the protagonist feels completely disillusioned and alone.

In the third part we witness Balbino's mistreatment of his wife and Dolorito's stay at La Mina, where he gains the confidence of his relative, Don Pedro Quiroga, and learns of the underground passageways in which a group of conspirators meets. Don Pedro's band of rebels is betrayed and denounced but Dolorito, on a mission in Loíza, attempting to recruit conspirators, escapes from the rural police thanks to the help of Pai Domingo, husband of the slave he had defended years before.

The following section sees Dolorito, now a more mature José Dolores, traveling throughout the island as an outlaw bandit, accompanied by Pai Domingo and joined by several other picturesque and picaresque characters whose stories are told. He leads them in activities and adventures to help the poor and downtrodden, with some notable triumphs, but his men are killed and he is imprisoned.

After seven years in prison, José Dolores, who now calls himself José Soler, decides to become a "man of the land" in the fifth and final part of the novel, but his plans yield to a return to rebellion when he learns that

Balbino Pasamonte's seventeen-year-old son has left Malén, Dolorito's favorite niece, pregnant. He is taken prisoner trying to avenge the wrong, but after three years manages to escape. Keeping the promise he had made to his mother twenty-five years before to donate a little gold leg to the Virgin of Monserrate in Hormigueros for his escaping from death as a small child, he observes the religious hypocrisy of the rich (Pasamonte) and sees Rosario, now married to a well-to-do man. José Dolores learns that his sister died in childbirth and that Juan Gorrión, popularly known as Juan Volao (*volado* means "flown" or "disappeared," in reference to his constant traveling), sings his legend in ballads throughout the island. After the American bombardment of Puerto Rico, seditious groups roam the island preying on ranchers, and while defending the life of his new boss, Don Álvaro Troche, José Dolores unwittingly kills Rosario's son, who was among the marauders. Rosario repudiates José Dolores completely and the latter realizes how much she has changed.

Feeling himself defeated in every way, José Dolores returns to Yukiyú and to his brother's house, finding that his enemy has already made friends with the new American masters. He fights Balbino Pasamonte, and as they struggle in the river into which they have fallen, José Dolores manages to drown him, thus repeating the feat of the Taíno chief Urayoán, who drowned the Spaniard Salcedo to prove that he was not an immortal god. A Texan friend of Balbino's shoots José Dolores, who drags himself into a cave where "no one can profane his death"(329).[3]

A Decisive Moment of History

As we have noted, *The Undertow* is the only novel in which Laguerre writes wholly about a historical moment he did not actually live, which Concha Meléndez calls "a decisive moment of our history."[4] As a historical novel, it is similar in plan to Pérez Galdós's *National Espisodes* in that a fictional protagonist is projected against important historical circumstance.[5] A detailed exposition of the history of the times would require more pages than could feasibly be dedicated to the task here; therefore we shall refer only to events which actually appear in the novel. The period covered may be considered a sort of parenthesis between two major events, the celebrated "Cry of Lares" and the change of sovereignty in 1898, roughly the last three decades of the nineteenth century.

Lares appears in Don Nicolás Velazco's irate allusions in the first part of the novel to the rebellion, which, he laments, went unpunished, for "he would have hanged each and every person responsible for the row in Lares" (50). He refers to events of the 23rd and 24th of September 1868, when a band of some 400 conspirators, poorly armed and trained, took the town of Lares without firing a shot and proclaimed the Republic of Puerto Rico. While proceeding to the town of San Sebastián, they were routed by superior Spanish military forces and those who could escape were pursued, captured, and sentenced to death, a fate averted by the dethronement of Queen Isabel II in Spain by "the Glorious Revolution of 1869" which saw the advent of a new Spanish government permitting the Puerto Ricans to form political parties and elect representatives to the *Cortes* ("Congress").[6] Don Álvaro Troche, for whom José Dolores works in the last part of *The Undertow,* had been imprisoned during Lares. The Cry of Lares became a watchword for the Puerto Rican cause and the Generation of the 1930s saw in it the birth of Puerto Rican consciousness. Lares is present in the very name of Dolorito (meaning "grief" or "pain") So*lares,* who lives under (*so* means "under") the influence of that important event. It is significant that when the protagonist leaves prison and resolves to become a farmer rather than return to a life of rebellion he assumes his maternal surname Soler, and that people insist on calling him Montojo because of his mysterious, legendary great-grandfather Carlos Montojo, suffocating the Solares name just as they do Dolorito's ideals when they deny him support because of fear of Spanish reprisals. In the little gold leg he wears as a medallion during his path around the island we are reminded of the heroine of Lares, Mariana Bracetti, called "Golden Arm," who fashioned the Lares banner.

In *The Undertow* historical dates are not given as such; references to historical happenings appear in the context of Dolorito's experience. We know, for example, that he was eleven years old before slavery was abolished (in 1873) because of the episode with the overseer and the slave. Abolition was accomplished after many years of struggle under the government of the First Spanish Republic, which liberalized many colonial policies and gave Puerto Rico a few years of respite, which had begun in 1869. This came to an end in 1875 with the return of the despotic governor General José Laureano Sanz, which in the novel is celebrated by three rural policemen who vow there will be no more mutinies like those which occurred in Yabucoa and Lares. With the Spanish Restoration, Sanz suspends constitutional guarantees, promulgates truculent decrees, and pursues teachers and reformists alike as separatists, as Laguerre states in his essay about Professor Labor Gómez's book on Sanz which appears in *Pulso de Puerto Rico, 1952–1954*. He further explains that public school teachers were a special target of Sanz's persecution: "It is one of the themes that my novel *The Undertow* treats. It was Sanz who instituted the rural police in Puerto Rico, of unfortunate remembrance."[7] We can therefore assume that the four years Dolorito studies under Don Cristo correspond to the relatively good times in Puerto Rico in the period from approximately 1870 to 1874 and that the subsequent persecution of both Don Cristo and his successor, Daniel Lugo, occurs in 1875. It is during this time that Don Felipe Santoro scorns the fallen Republic responsible for the abolition of slavery, but assures Balbino that an astute man can always find new slaves to serve him. The rural police install their headquarters in Monte Grande, Dolorito and Pasamonte meet for the first time, and the latter begins his ascent to power.

The six years Dolorito spends at La Mina make him aware of the efforts of conspirators against Spanish oppression who, under increased vigilance by the authorities, find it difficult to operate. Their underground nature is aptly symbolized by the group which meets in the subterranean passages of the old mine.

The next important date which may be identified from developments in the novel is the "terrible year of '87" as it is popularly known. Laguerre, commenting upon a book by Antonio Rivera treating the last years of the Spanish regime on the island in *Pulse of Puerto Rico*, provides the following description of events:

> In 1887 a Puerto Rican Economic Society is founded to boycott Spanish commerce. Secret societies are founded. The Autonomist leaders—Labra, Baldorioty, Cepeda—never rest. The autonomist assembly of 1887 in Ponce had a great deal of resonance. And the Componte [infamous marauding bands of rural police which dragged Puerto Ricans from their homes] arrives in that same year, "terrible year."[8]

An Important Period of History

This is obviously the time in the novel when Dolorito, already famous as a bandit, keeps away from Yukiyú after an unsuccessful incursion into Monte Grande. His plans are changed, however, because General Palacio's "police were very active in the countryside of the Island. Everywhere they pursued the members of a supposed secret society" (240). For this reason the jíbaros of Cidra distrust Dolorito and his men. Precisely when General Palacio directs acts of despotism and *Componte* from Aibonito and "the Island was a boiling pot of turmoil" (257), José Dolores carries out one of his most spectacular feats upon freeing old Ño Segundo from the rural police and obliging the wealthy young man who fathered the son of Ño Segundo's granddaughter to marry her. Reference is made in the novel to the jailing of autonomist leaders after their meeting in Ponce. Dolorito's fortune also declines as his men die from disease or are killed and he himself is imprisoned trying to escape to Cuba to help in that country's revolution.

Dolorito's unintentional violence against Rosario's son is set after the United States takeover of Puerto Rico and his return to his brother's house after the destructive hurricane, (San Ciríaco) which would place the action after August 1899. Surprisingly there is no mention at all of the fact that Spain finally granted autonomy to Puerto Rico in 1897, autonomy that was initiated only months before the American arrival. It is strange that Laguerre, who is always so attentive to irony, omits reference to this fact. We believe that the omission responds to Laguerre's desire to avoid romanticizing Spain's action or attributing it to any magnanimity on her part, since the gesture of allowing autonomy was motivated by United States pressure and, in any case, it never had a chance to function.[9] The situation is, however, recreated symbolically in José Dolores's victory over the Spaniard Balbino Pasamonte followed immediately by his being dealt a mortal blow by the latter's American hunting companion. Dolorito's aspirations seem silenced forever, and yet they are not, like the voice of the underground river heard in the cave which is his final resting place, for his feat was a repetition of that of Urayoán centuries before and in the same manner may be repeated in the future.

The undertow of history is seen in reference to the situation of the indigenous Taíno heroes confronting the Spanish conquest in the sixteenth century. Dolorito always returns to the mist-covered Yukiyú (a Taíno word from which *Luquillo* probably derived, here referring to El Yunque), where he hears the voice of Yukiyú, "benign god of the simple indigenous mythology" (317). Another allusion to these times is the term *Becerrillo,* by which Dolorito refers to Balbino, for a footnote explains that this was the name of a famous dog which helped the Spaniards' colonization of the island. Pasamonte likewise helps the colonial authorities and shifts allegiance quite easily to the new masters. The quest for gold, which in small quantities the poverty-stricken peasants manage to separate from the waters of the river in order to buy some necessities, also recalls the Spaniards' aspirations in the sixteenth century. The most important colonial event is recreated in Dolorito's drowning of Pasamonte in the chapter entitled "The Immortals Perish in the River." The drowning of the Spaniard Diego Salcedo was ordered by the Taíno Chief Urayoán in order to prove the mortality of the invader "gods" in 1511.

Historical Legacy

Laguerre uses historical material because of its impact upon the present and future. We may well ask the same questions he poses in *Pulse of Puerto Rico* after reading Labor Gómez's history of the same period which is that of *The Undertow.* Reading "Laguerre" in place of "Gómez" presents the reader of the novel with an important challenge:

> What significance does the historical moment which Gómez examines in his work have on our Puerto Rican life? What resonances did it leave in our conscience? What effect has it had on our subsequent collective conduct?[10]

The novels Laguerre writes after *The Undertow* are in fact a fictional attempt to answer these questions, but since the book was presented to Puerto Rican readers in 1949, it seems likely that he perceived some similarities between the mid-1940s and the historical juncture portrayed in his novel. For Zayas Micheli the link is Laguerre's disillusionment with the Popular Democratic party, which changed its course from seeking independence to interior autonomy, prompting a group of dissidents to separate and form the Puerto Rican Independence party.[11] Concha Meléndez says the title of *The Undertow* symbolically expresses the retrogression of the idea of revolution.[12] Most critics tend to interpret the book more as a political novel than a historical one, finding a parallel between the death of Dolorito and the abandonment of the independence ideal by the majority party. This is only partly correct and in any case simplistic, leaving as many doubts as it does answers.

A brief summary of Puerto Rico's history in the first half of this century is in order. With the granting of United States citizenship Puerto Ricans were drafted into service in the First World War. The island was hard hit by the Great Depression and in the 1930s there was a good deal of political violence and general desperation. Then in 1940 a new party, the Popular Democratic party, led by Luis Muñoz Marín, came into power amid much expectation and proceeded to undertake agrarian reform, the creation of new service agencies, and industrialization. In 1946 the United States named a Puerto Rican as governor of the island for the first time and the following year permitted popular election of governor, setting Puerto Rico on the road to autonomy, but not independence, as some had expected, finding an alternative in the Independence party. It was a time for examination of conscience, to recall Puerto Rican aspirations repressed in the previous century and frustrated in this one, but also a time to consider the pressing economic, social, and educational needs which the Popular party promised to meet and had in fact taken measures to correct. For us *The Undertow* responds to this difficult predicament by examining *differences,* as well as similarities, between the Spanish domination and the contemporary American presence, while at the same time expressing disappointment at not seeing the aspirations for independence fulfilled. This would make it a much more thematically complex novel than a politically oriented reading would reveal.

One perplexing aspect of the novel, in that there is no comparable situation in 1946, is the atmosphere of severe repression in the Spanish-dominated Puerto Rico of the previous century, with the closing of public schools, arbitrary laws, the *compontes,* and unlimited powers of the abusive rural police. Some observations Laguerre offers in his master's degree thesis *Modernist Poetry in Puerto Rico,* presented in 1942 and published in 1969, may illuminate this:

> There is no doubt that the war of '98 influenced subsequent Modernist poetry; hence the great number of poems with political motives in the beginning of this century. Resentment toward Spain provoked by the war of independence turns into love and nostalgia for the former Mother Country.[13]

This idea appears again in the book in a specifically Puerto Rican context and in the aforementioned essay "The Times of Governor Sanz": "The truth is that our Nineteenth Century is far from the resplendent golden age tht the exaggerated ingenuousness of some few would like us to see."[14]

The vivid atmosphere of repression reproduced in *The Undertow* is intended to oppose any tendency to romanticize or idealize the "good old days" of the Spanish presence as a reaction to any disappointment regarding Puerto Rico's political status. There is certainly nothing desirable about grinding poverty, child mortality, or death from hunger, in addition to notorious abuses inspired by unconditional despotism. Laguerre seems to propose a sensible and realistic alternative, a Puerto Rican consciousness which can find inspiration in its indigenous past and its native history and does not have to rely upon a romanticized and false view of Spanish Puerto Rico to present its credentials for maintaining an identity different from that of the Americans.

Another difficult point to resolve is why Laguerre presents Dolorito Montojo as a bandit and outlaw rather than as the paradigm of a revolutionary hero. His brief career as a conspirator ends when the rural police jail Don Pedro Quiroga. As Daniel Lugo had casually suggested, he becomes a bandit, so that the political rebellion is essentially replaced by broader programs involving stealing from the rich to give to the poor, defending women, and correcting moral wrongs, adding economic, social, and ethical dimensions to the mature José Dolores. Laguerre makes it clear that his protagonist is not a political rebel: "if he had been a revolutionary leader, José Dolores would not have had scruples: he would have killed and set fire to contribute to the freedom of his Island" (239). He is determined not to kill and only does so at the very end in mortal struggle with his arch-enemy Balbino Pasamonte. Instead of taking on the whole Spanish government, he takes on those who victimize the poor and defenseless on a smaller, more limited scale. The opening sentences of the novel announce the contradictions in his spirit between the desire for adventures and that of tilling the land. After his first imprisonment, José Dolores returns to the latter, but, as Concha Meléndez puts it, he is "'the man of the land' who has no land to stay on."[15] Only in utter desperation is he capable of avenging the dispossessed and the imprisoned by killing Balbino Pasamonte, "a hateful symbol of injustice and oppression" (323). The revolutionary of former days at La Mina only reappears at the end, the lone revolutionary who kills a symbol and becomes one, only to sink into the mist of Yukiyú and of legend. The events of 1946 are not comparable to those which drive José Dolores to his ultimate act, but the end is clear regarding the submission to "false gods," be they Spanish or American.

The Aura of Legend

In an essay entitled "History and Legend," which appears in *Pulse of Puerto Rico,* Laguerre affirms the importance of legend which is for him "the leavening of history":

In all parts of the world, when one learns his people's history, it is reinforced with interpretations more or less legendary or mythical. Historical events in themselves lack popular appeal. They attract interest when they are saturated with legend.[16]

Several characters in *The Undertow* are surrounded by the aura of legend, such as Dolorito's great-grandfather Carlos Montojo, former owner of La Mina, who committed suicide. Ironically the good man that was Carlos Montojo disappeared only to have legend portray him as the devil's ally who "not content to profane religion, carried on impious conspirations against Spain and its august monarchs" (29). Under the mystique of the Montojo legend people insist on using the surname "Montojo" for the Solares family (Don Carlos was Dolorito's *maternal* grandfather). Dolorito grows up hearing the legends about his forbear and "as he grew in experiences, the fear of Don Carlos was transforming itself into a mixture of admiration and ineffable mystery" (29).

Dolorito's second encounter with a personage of popular conjecture is with Don Pedro Quiroga, also a relative, who occupies La Mina and shows the same inclinations toward rebellion against the established norms as Don Carlos Montojo. He takes full advantage of the mystery and superstition already associated with La Mina to make sure he is undisturbed there in order to carry out his conspirations. He attempts to scare Dolorito with the clanking of chains and reappearing suddenly in different places, which, as the young man later discovers, is facilitated by secret passageways. With the imprisonment of Don Pedro and the burning of La Mina by Pasamonte to "purify" the "accursed" hacienda, the aura of legend is conferred upon Dolorito in the fourth part of the novel, when accompanied by Lázaro Cuevas, alias "the Magician," and Sandalio Cortijo, "the Phantasm," he becomes known and feared as a bandit.

A similar process of rising to the category of a legend takes place in the novel *Montoya Plantation,* whose title in Spanish, *Solar Montoya,* seems suggested in reverse in the surnames of Dolorito *Montojo Solares,* for in *The Undertow* the conversion of the protagonist into a legend follows a somewhat inverse process. In Laguerre's earlier novel Don Alonso Montoya progressively enters the realm of legend and myth and at the end becomes pure legend. In *The Undertow* Dolorito's fame as a bandit culminates in the fourth part, after which he becomes progressively more detached from that legend, more depressed by his human condition, more vulnerable to defeat. He sees his own legend as something separated from his present self and renounces it to try to become José Soler. At the close of the novel, however, he recaptures his legend in a final act of heroism which links him to Taíno legend, the feat of Urayoán. Struggling in the river against Balbino Pasamonte, he swims against the undertow of colonial oppression (his ability as a swimmer is stressed) and becomes part of a native legend that lives on.

The first act which associates Dolorito with heroes is his defense of the slave woman against the overseer at the age of eleven. Critics have failed to recognize this as an allusion to the feat of the biblical Moses who strikes a mortal blow to a taskmaster beating a weary Hebrew slave mercilessly and because of this becomes an outlaw. Also like Moses, who as a male Hebrew baby was condemned to die in the waters of the Nile but was fortunately saved by Pharaoh's daughter, Dolorito miraculously escapes death as an infant, inspiring his mother's promise to give a tiny golden leg to the Virgin of Monserrate. These similarities make even more ironic the differences in their respective destinies. Dolorito never realizes Moses' accomplishment in leading his people to freedom and a promised land. With his Mount Sinai in Yukiyú, he is doomed to a peripatetic existence in the wilderness, but, like Moses, his final resting place is an unknown cave.

It is interesting to note that mountains have long been associated with greatness and legend from earliest antiquity, such as Mount Sinai, the Mount of Jesus' sermon, and Mount Olympus of Greek mythology. The antagonists of *The Undertow* and their home bases relate directly to mountains. The word *monte* ("mount") is suggested in both surnames, *Mont*ojo and Pasa*monte;* the first finds strength in the mountain enveloped in mist, Yukiyú, while the second makes his kingdom in Monte Grande (literally large or great mountain), but his greatness is spurious.

Further biblical suggestion links José Dolores with the Old Testament Joseph (José) who is placed in a pit (akin to the abandoned well in *The Undertow*) by his envious brothers and whose chastity, like that of José Dolores, is legendary. There is even a hint of a feared Potiphar's wife episode when Don Pedro's maiden sister arrives from Spain, showing dislike toward Dolorito while evidently inviting his attention. This is not to deny, of course, a similarity also to Don Quijote, whose chastity, as Zayas Micheli points out, was inspired by a pure and ideal love.[17]

In José Dolores's career as a bandit, defying authority since he is unable to destroy it and stealing from the rich to give to the poor, there are echoes of the English folk hero Robin Hood, the late-fourteenth or early-fifteenth-century outlaw who lived and poached in the king's forest, Sherwood, championing the cause of the poor and oppressed against those who represented the power of government. His comrades were known as the "merry men," a title which may likewise apply to Dolorito's picaresque companions. Lázaro Cuevas specializes in making the dead talk by tying a string to the corpse's toe under the covers to make him move and by having an accomplice supply the voice. Dolorito extracts a very appropriate parallel; if Cuevas wants to join him, he'll have to make another type of dead people talk—the hungry who don't move. The other "merry man" is Sandalio Cortijo, who plays ghost in order to steal food and assure himself an abandoned house in which to live. This too contains a message: "After all, it is more worth while to be a phantasm than a man on this island" (215). During a *baquiné* (celebration with song and dance held by the ex-slaves when a child dies) they make the dead child "move" with the cord, a trick to steal the roast pig during the ensuing tumult, to the dismay of José Dolores, who has imposed strict rules of conduct on his men. At the *baquiné,* Pai Domingo hears his deeds celebrated in songs that portray him as a hero and already-legendary figure.

José Dolores, latterday Robin Hood of Puerto Rico, marauding in the area around Yukiyú and in other parts of the island, realizes some successes. Like Don Quijote in the second part of Cervantes's novel and Martín Fierro in the second part of José Hernández's poem, he is surprised to learn that he is well known. He is successful in freeing a captive from two policemen and in freeing Ño Segundo, a helpless old man accused of stealing a cow from the powerful Don Modesto because he could not bear to see his granddaughter and her baby starve. He uses to his advantage the legends that have sprung up around him in order to intimidate Don Modesto and make his son Carlos marry Ño Segundo's granddaughter in accordance with his moral responsibility as father of the child.

The final part of the novel contrasts the man who after seven years of prison is "without a present or a future" with legend portraying him as "almost an immaterial being" (285). When a jíbaro tells him about Juan Volao's *décimas* celebrating the bandit Dolorito Montojo, the latter contemplates his legend as something unreal: "It is as if I read it in a book" (298). He is a lonely hero but thanks to the *décimas* of Juan Volao (and the novel of Laguerre) he gains the popular appeal and support he could not gain in real life. If stories of the miracles of the Virgin of Monserrate have inspired popular enthusiasm for three centuries, as the novel shows, perhaps the legend of Dolorito Montoya may some day provide inspiration too for the causes he espoused. The end of the novel underscores the eternal character of myth: "Outside, between the mists of the Yukiyú, his fable remained alive. The best part of his existence belonged to the future" (329).

Dolorito Montojo's legendary dimension is easily accepted by the reader due to the narrative style, which, in contrast to other Laguerrean novels, avoids giving us access to the protagonist's inner thoughts. We are limited basically to observing his actions and dialogue with others, together with the narrator's indications. José Dolores speaks and acts in a novel of action rather than of meditation or introspection, so that there is always some distance between the protagonist and the reader, a distance which favors legend and myth.

A Pervasive Evil

The underlying theme of *The Undertow* is a universal one, oppression and how it pervades and eats at the very fiber of all sectors of life. The oppression which exists on the national level with absolutely no regard for justice or human rights breeds oppression in economic and moral contexts. The repression carried out by the Spanish governor, rural police, and *compontes* creates an atmosphere symbolized in the well of still and fetid waters into which Dolorito falls. It is clear that Dolorito Montojo never escapes from the well of injustices, persecutions, and abuses during his life.

The oppressive pattern introduces itself early in the novel in the institution of slavery. The beating of a slave is particularly repugnant because the victim is a pregnant woman who had stolen a codfish, from hunger. By the time Dolorito meets Pai Domingo in Loíza, slavery had been abolished, but the lasting effects are still visible in the improvised way the ex-slaves live.

Father-son relationships also repeat the oppressive model, as can be observed in the despotic manner in which Dolorito's godfather Cristino treats his son Juan Gorrión and punishes his children constantly. In spite of this situation, Juan's innately happy spirit maintains him singing, since "birds are no less so for being caged" (18; *gorrión* means "sparrow").

The worst lot in such a repressive society fell to women. Cristino brings up his daughter Rosario in typical despotic fashion:

Beginning when Sarito was only fourteen years old the father began to put into practice the famous educative methods that Spanish tradition dispenses to women: absolutely no contacts with men, long dresses. . . . Ah, sir, woman is very weak and compromises man: lucky that Sarito was going to grow up among many brothers! (18)

The customary frugality of the country folk is not practiced by the husband, who reserves the best of provisions and treats for himself. Since Cristino had a weakness for women, he projects his own experience upon Rosarito, keeping her virtually a prisoner in the home basing his rights to run her life for her on the fact that she owes her existence to him. (It may be said that Spanish governmental authority was based on a similar premise.) The disastrous effects of such upbringing are evident in Rosario's being seduced and abandoned by the experienced rural policeman Gil Borjes. Even when paternal authority is lax, women like Lina and Rosa, Dolorito's mother and sister, are "slaves" of the home because of extreme poverty.

The most impressive case of individual autocracy is, of course, Balbino Pasamonte, whom Don Pedro Quiroga calls "a despot in miniature," proposing the following parallel:

What wouldn't he do if instead of being a simple boss in Monte Grande he were governor of the Island? Look at how Balbino Pasamonte acts and you will see an example of how the Government acts. Monte Grande looks like a small laboratory of all the evil the Government of kings and despots does. (172)

Expropriating land and treating his peons badly are some of the evils he perpetrates, but the height of Pasamonte's perverseness is the martyrdom he inflicts upon his wife, Lucía, in perpetual punishment for having loved Lorenzo Quiroga. In a boudoir scene, highly unusual in Laguerre's fiction, Balbino actually rapes his wife, whose growing hatred of him responds to physical and mental abuse. He alienates their son from her, telling the boy stories in which he alludes to his conquest of Monte Grande and Lucía and inculcating in the child the same traits which make him repulsive. Even if Lucía's father had not gone back to Spain her plight would be the same, for "Don Nicolás was tradition in person, a horrible tradition that always manifested itself against women" (150). The despotism of the father is substituted by that of the husband.

José Dolores's speech and directives in defense of women are, as Zayas Micheli notes, reminiscent of Don Quijote's attitude, and point out the pressing need for reform. He would put an end to the victimization of women, seeing in all women an image of his mother. Even though individual female characters are not as extensively developed in *The Undertow* as some male characters, the plights of Lina, Rosario, the daughter of Ño Segundo, and Malén combine to form a strong denunciation of oppression. What drives José Dolores to his "semidivine" mission against Balbino Pasamonte at the end of the novel is the desire to avenge what the young Arturo Pasamonte had done to Malén. The correction of injustice exemplified in his previous success in arranging the marriage of Ño Segundo's granddaughter belongs to his legendary past; Dolorito is no longer able to realize the same feat, yet his heroism achieves even greater proportions.

Thus despotism proceeding from the Spanish crown's representatives reflects itself in social, familial, and economic relationships. For Don Pedro Quiroga "the evil resides in the colonial system" (157). Governors Sanz and Palacio mistreat the Puerto Ricans as the overseer does the slave, the landowner his peons, fathers their sons and daughters, and husbands their wives. Despotism is an all-pervasive evil which must be alleviated by the true spirit of republic, not only on the national level but also at home, on the farm, and in the school.

Education and the Future

The second part of *The Undertow* is largely the portrayal of educational experiences of a varying nature revealing Laguerre's great concern for youth. When several years later he offers education as the greatest interest of the Puerto Ricans in general he clearly acknowledges it as his own. Several teachers appear in the novel, some formal schoolmasters, others informal tutors and parents; all have very definite impact upon their charges.

Dolorito's first teacher is Don Cristo, a liberal who sees all Puerto Rico as well into which Dolorito had fallen. With his eyes toward Yukiyú, he dreams of a fount that will cure all evils. He attributes man's perdition to the sense of property and would establish a republic in the Yukiyú. Dolorito serves this humble man with great dedication and is deeply hurt when the school is closed because, as Don Cristo says, "they have heard me speak of a Republic of mists" (107), recalling for the reader the experience of his namesake. With innocent fervor Dolorito proposes to his beloved teacher that they go to live in the Yukiyú. The four years he spends under Don Cristo's guidance not only teach him to read and write, but also to dream. In the repressive and stifling atmosphere of the island, Don Cristo can only die of hunger and starvation, which surely is as much spiritual as physical.

Perhaps the fictional character of Don Cristóbal Amorós, whose name suggests both Christ and love *(amor),* is patterned after the famous nineteenth-century schoolmaster Rafael Cordero Molina, who became a legend in his own right, a shoemaker by profession who offered free schooling to poor children. His students included the patriots José Julián Acosta, Alejandro Tapia y Rivera, and Ramón Baldorioty de Castro.[18] A famous painting of him by Francisco Oller may be found today in the *Ateneo Puertorriqueño* ("Puerto Rican Athenaeum") in San Juan. Perhaps even the name Don Cristo harbors a reflection of the surname *Cordero* ("lamb"), since the latter is often associated with Christ. Don Cristo has an elevating influence on the mind of Dolorito, sowing in his heart seeds of social justice which later bloom in his program as a bandit to share the wealth of the rich with the poor.

Daniel Lugo, the schoolmaster who takes Don Cristo's place, is more realistic and practical than his predecessor, declaring all his students "companions" and creating a republic right in the classroom. When a disorderly student disturbs the class he is considered nonexistent and is ignored by the group. In one humorous episode, a disruptive offender is declared "dead" and a funeral takes place around him. Lugo's teaching is not limited to class days; he takes the children on excursions Saturdays. He manages to eat better than Don Cristo by having the pupils bring in samples of chickens and turbercules for study; naturally he keeps them for his own consumption. Although Dolorito is not a student of Lugo, he does have the opportunity to observe a miniature republic in action. When the schoolmaster is vanquished by the calumnies of Balbino Pasamonte and Gil Borjes, he confides in Dolorito, "Where can one go without finding people like Gil Borjes? One has to live like an outlaw in his own land. I think one could gain more by becoming a bandit" (130). Now, "for the first time in his life, Dolorito began to doubt that one could live like Don Cristo wished to" (131). He watches the "republic" of Daniel Lugo's creation fall, carried away by the undertow of oppression.

The third "educator" in this second part of the novel, Don Felipe Santoro, becomes so quite by accident. This "model of Spanish nobility was sex from head to foot, an implacable inciter of original sin" (81). When a rustic relative, the sixteen-year-old Balbino Pasamonte, is sent to him from Spain, the old bachelor decides to act out the farce of teaching the ingenuous bumpkin courtly language in order to impress "his majesty" Don Nicolás Velazco. When he sees how eagerly his pupil responds to his lessons, Don Felipe enthusiastically tutors him in his philosophy of life and in the process shows increasing signs of eccentricity, which later culminate in his suicide. He instructs Balbino in the art of taking advantage of others' weaknesses. His precepts involve keeping a tight reign on Lucía, who, he insists, will be Balbino's wife; committing abuses, always with valid pretexts in the name of government, church, or public order; becoming a friend of the Church; ceding momentarily, if necessary, to triumph in the long run; making others serve him; and staying on top always.

The cynical nature of Don Felipe Santoro is very similar to that of the unforgettable Vizcacha, who, in the second part of José Hernández's *Martín Fierro,* assumes the role of tutor of Fierro's Second Son, advising him to defend his own skin first, become a friend of judges and authority, be wary of women, feed himself at others' expense, and fight only when he is ready to win. Both sets of recommendations are alike in tone and content, suggesting that the picturesque and eccentric character of Laguerre's creation may be inspired by Vizcacha. Both tutors illustrate their recommendations with graphic references to ranch life, animals, and popular sayings. Vizcacha, for example, advises, "Never decide to stay / where you see skinny dogs"; "what man most needs / to have / according to how I see it / is the memory of the burro / who never forgets where he eats."[19] Santoro, although he is not a rancher, resorts to the same type of imagery: "You will always be mounted. The whip is not for the horse but for you" (88); "the young mare is always cross until she becomes accustomed to the saddle" (85). The advice of Vizcacha contrasts with another set of precepts enunciated by the hero Martín Fierro, who extolls hard work, self-respect, family unity, obedience, respect for women, and avoidance of killing, robbing, and getting drunk. A similar contrast in *The Undertow* may be adduced from the teachings of Don Cristo, opposed to those of Don Felipe, and later from the teachings of Dolorito himself. For Don Cristo "life is in *being,* not in *being somewhere"* (100). Don Felipe is a lot more cynical and dangerous than his Argentine counterpart Vizcacha, whose concern is surviving in the pampa, for his precepts, aimed at getting ahead and controlling others, are filled with lessons in hypocrisy and perverseness. What began as a joke takes on great seriousness as Balbino is schooled in all he needs to know to assault the "castle" of Nicolás Velazco to become lord of Monte Grande and carry out to the letter the lessons of life learned from his tutor. Balbino's Machiavellian education is eminently successful in a society which demands Machiavellian behavior.

Another informal teacher appears in the third part of the novel in the person of Don Pedro Quiroga, from whom Dolorito learns resentment toward governmental authority, in opposition to Don Cristo's admonition against hating one's enemies. He also learns to overcome weakness of will, which for Don Pedro is the collective defect of the Puerto Rican, to make use of superstition and mystery to harass authorities, and finally to work for a republic of free men instead of dreaming of Don Cristo's republic made of mist.

The importance of education is consistently underscored in *The Undertow* because the student later becomes a teacher. Balbino Pasamonte tutors his son with stories of Pedro Animala ("a folkloric character representing the astute man without scruples," 149) and takes advantage of the child's innocence to inculcate in him perverse attitudes. It is no wonder that the father is delighted to hear years later that his son, at the age of seventeen years, has accomplished the great exploit of leaving Malén pregnant. Thanks to such assiduous teachings, moral evils are perpetuated from one generation to another in receptive individuals, leaving a legacy which hopefully can be overcome by teachers of another sort, be they fictional or real, like Don Cristo, Daniel Lugo, Rafael Cordero, and Enrique Laguerre.

Chapter Six
The Wandering Puerto Rican

Laguerre's novels *La ceiba en el tiesto* [The Ceiba Tree in the Flower Pot], completed in New York in the summer of 1954 and published two years later, and *El laberinto* [The Labyrinth], published in New York in 1959 and in English translation the following year, portray the wandering Puerto Rican. Both novels, whose titles suggest confinement, depict the Puerto Rican experience extending beyond the island scenario to the United States mainland and other countries. The author's trips to New York between 1952 and 1959, a period in which emigration increased considerably, undoubtedly provided material for these books.

The Ceiba Tree in the Flower Pot

Protagonist Gustavo Vargas narrates his story, which begins with his involvement in a Patriotic Conjunction plot to assassinate an important person, but he cannot bring himself to carry out the order. Interspersed in the narration are recollections of his estranged wife, who led him into the radical group; incidents of losing his memory; days of peace at *Playa Rosada* ("Rose-colored Beach") with Uncle Leoncio, who taught him to love nature; his humble mother, the "Indian" Tule, and the legend of a father he didn't know; and being forced to leave his native *Pueblo* ("Town") with his paternal uncle, the lawyer Matienzo, to live with his sanctimonious aunts in *Río Loco* ("(Mad River").

Convinced that he is being pursued for his defection, Gustavo returns to his boyhood refuge at Playa Rosada and Pueblo and then flees to New York to lose himself in the anonymity of the metropolis, where he keeps to himself with a minimum of human contacts. Doña María, the mother of two Puerto Rican co-workers who live apart from the "colony" in New York, remarks that she feels like a ceiba tree in a flower pot, referring to the gigantic native tree which, uprooted and confined, would surely wither away. When personal relations get complicated, Gustavo runs away and begins a decline which leads him to the Bowery until a Puerto Rican whom he has asked for money makes him feel ashamed of his degradation. He takes a job painting windows on a skyscraper, contemplates suicide, but desists and returns to Puerto Rico to help a friend, Don José, in a campaign for education and social reform. Back in Pueblo Gustavo is invited by Juan Lorenzi to join his fishing business, but he prefers to serve as secretary and public relations man for Javier Aguirre, a politician of the majority party in San Juan, thus entering "false worlds" in which personal economic security comes first. His dissatisfaction prompts another flight to New York. He is drafted into service in the army, after which he travels with the merchant marine to Gulf ports and Europe, which he finds depressing. Gustavo returns to Puerto Rico, commits himself to a sanatorium, and begins his rehabilitation, going back to Playa Rosada. In Pueblo he finds that Juan Lorenzi has imprisoned a barracuda that was responsible for taking the leg of Julio Antonio Cruzado, Gustavo's old comrade from the Patriotic Conjunction, recently released from prison for his part in the aborted assassination attempt. Gustavo joins the fishing cooperative with his boyhood friend Juan Pitirre and marries his old sweetheart Elisa, finding peace in the simple life, the company of humble villagers, and closeness to nature.

The Ceiba Tree in the Flower Pot is one of the first novelistic portrayals of life in New York for the Puerto Rican, preceded by Guillermo Cotto-Thorner's novel *Trópico en Manhattan* [Tropic in Manhattan], published three years before, in 1951. Unlike the characters in Cotto-Thorner's book, Gustavo never really intends to adapt himself to life in the metropolis but rather considers it a crossroads where he comes to ask himself who he is and where he is going. He is disturbed by the sensation of anonymity, as well as by prejudice, job discrimination, the mechanization and artificiality which alienate man from nature, the dark subway tunnels and the blinding lights of Times Square, and Coney Island—"a compendium of all that is morbid and unhealthy" (554).[1] In spite of these general views of the city, however, Gustavo's experiences are in large measure atypical, since he avoids mixing with his compatriots, imagining himself pursued by the Patriotic Conjunction. The family of Doña María is not part of the Puerto Rican "colony" and another acquaintance, Joe McAdams, who seems to be a blond American prejudiced toward Puerto Ricans, turns out to be none other than José García McAdams of the Patriotic Conjunction. Even Gustavo's experience as a Bowery bum is atypical, for as a Puerto Rican passerby berates him: "Leave here. This is for Americans. Our poverty is of a different sort" (564). Like a Jonah emerging from the belly of the whale, he leaves the "large intestine" of New York to begin his rehabilitation.

As a wandering Puerto Rican Gustavo is very aware of a plurality of worlds. Indeed a word which appears with notable frequency in the novel is "world." There is the protective world of Pueblo with Uncle Leoncio and the "Indian" Tule; that of Bahía Honda, where his lawyer uncle entertains himself with the international set; that of his refuge Playa Rosada; that of politics and radicalism; and the hostile world of New York. Lorenzi's preferred world is the sea because it gives him the illusion of total freedom; Julio Antonio Cruzado lives in "another world" of pirates, hidden treasures that could finance a revolution, and epic deeds. Gustavo chooses the world in which he will live, Playa Rosada, but he has the ability to maintain friendships with those whose worlds are different, like Lorenzi, Cruzado, and even Aguirre, with tolerance for others in "a wide world in which we all fit if we want to" (621).

These worlds are often in conflict, on the local and on the international levels, and Gustavo laments living in a century of great conflict. If Teófilo Sampedro's problem in *The 30th of February* was basically existential, Gustavo Vargas's dilemma is even more complex since it is "co-existential." Driven to the verge of suicide, he realizes that Hamlet's alternatives to be or not to be are more complicated in Spanish, where being is rendered by two verbs: *ser* and *estar*. His problem from the opening chapter is with *estar*, concerned with conditions subject to change and with alignment, because he is called upon to be with one group or another, to affiliate and commit himself to carry out a plot which threatens his *ser*, or existence. This is reflected on the international level in the World War in which he is obligated to take part and which he simply calls a "hell" with no further description of the experience. He feels himself controlled, unable to make his own decisions and direct his own life, but comes to realize that in a world of wars and partisanship, one must begin in some way and in some place, so he begins from his corner of the world in the company of friends, family, and humble folk.

What Gustavo learns is presented toward the end of the novel virtually in the form of recommendations, some appearing in italics as expressions of his conscience. Although he is a highly individualized protagonist (a funny madman, he says), the lessons he learns have a clearly collective message: *"The first step in understanding others is to try to understand oneself"* (611). "*Small acts of solidarity, anonymous, sincere, repeated, succeed in alleviating conflicts. . . .* We cannot evade living our times, though we live with simplicity. . . . (612) *This carrying out of small acts, moment by moment, to dignify our existence, is what builds the foundations of the land*" (613). "It is essential to eliminate the germ of disaffection here, in every one of the places that together form the sum of the world. . . . There is no way to conquer freedom other than acts of togetherness" (622). The first-person narrative is very important in that these recommendations, which would be artistically intolerable as a direct expression of the author's views, are acceptable in the context of the protagonist's experience as the vital lessons he has learned.

Puerto Rican critics such as Francisco Arriví, René Marqués, Concha Meléndez, José Juan Beauchamp, and Luis O. Zayas Micheli agree that the novel treats the theme of the collective Puerto Rican conscience seeking freedom from colonialism, but do not relate it to its historical circumstance.[2] Zayas Micheli does point out that the Patriotic Conjunction is related to the Nationalist leader Albizu Campos's revolutionary program and that this was a period of weakening of the Independence movement, but the fact is that in the years preceding the completion of the novel, some very important events and changes had taken place: 1950 was a year of tremendous political turmoil, with a Nationalist attempt to assassinate the first elected native governor, Luis Muñoz Marín, in the Fortaleza, the official residence. This was followed by a shooting incident in the United States House of Representatives in the proximity of President Truman, after which Albizu Campos was imprisoned, precipitating the demise of the Nationalist party. In 1952 the Commonwealth of Puerto Rico was inaugurated and its Constitution adopted by general plebiscite amid general optimism. The Popular party, under the leadership of Muñoz Marín, a master politician and statesman, set about to deal with social and economic problems, leaving the always-candescent issue of status in the background.[3]

I believe that *The Ceiba Tree in the Flower Pot* is largely a response to these events, for the end of the novel suggests a spirit of reconciliation, hope, and the desirability of working toward badly needed social reform by means of common effort from the grass roots rather than political chicanery or radicalism. Julio Antonio Cruzado ("Crusader"), whose epic ideals commit him to revolution, is shot down. Lorenzi, the loner, whose dream is complete individual freedom (hardly possible, says Gustavo, pointing out his creditors), leaves the island to hunt in Africa. Gustavo contemplates their disappearance with sadness but is optimistic about the future. Of course, as Tomás Navarro Tomás and later Beauchamp allege, there is always the possibility of new disturbances in this paradisiacal peace found in his rose-colored beach, but that is a characteristic of life itself.[4] I feel that Laguerre's attitude toward the betterment of life in Puerto Rico is one of guarded optimism. Perhaps the events of those years inspired his hopes that with each one doing his part the wandering Puerto Rican might really find a home in his homeland. The problem is to refuse to let politics turn into a religion, to keep the being of *ser* before that of *estar,* or taking sides. Laguerre, of course, does not tell us all this directly, but it is implicit in the happy ending of his novel.

As we have come to expect in Laguerre, there is a good deal of symbolism in the novel, perhaps even more than usual. Most metaphors involve allusions to flora and fauna in keeping with the protagonist's fondness for nature. The metaphoric title has been the object of critical discussion since René Marqués observed that Doña María's comment about feeling like a ceiba tree in a flower pot referring to the Puerto Rican emigration ("It hurts to have to live far from our country. We no longer fit in it" [553]) does not seem complete enough to entitle the whole novel. Francisco Arriví's interpretation that the flower pot is Puerto Rico itself is supported by José Juan Beauchamp.[5] I too subscribe to this view but would go beyond, for Laguerre tends to use clusters of related metaphors applicable to several situations, as in *The Fingers of the Hand,* where both fingers and hands form a constellation of connotations. So too in *The Ceiba Tree in the Flower Pot* there are a number of associated metaphors suggestive of confinement and suffocation, beginning early in the book with Vargas's nightmare in which he feels himself being encased in a coffin, reflecting his distaste for being controlled by others. Another similar image is the spider's web, for José García is described as a spider in his ability to escape on a thread, and Javier Aguirre weaves "little intellectual traps." The commercial trawl or dragnet that indiscriminately captures fish and the enclosure which torments the barracuda may also be considered related symbols that complement the novel's title.

Laguerre's symbols are clearly underscored but nevertheless radiate innumerable conjectures applicable to characters and situations other than those which are explicitly mentioned. Beauchamp, for example, sees in the barracuda episode Lorenzi's adventurous spirit restrained by the island world, Julio Antonio's frustrated epic dreams, and Gustavo's limitations which inhibit all potential ferocity. Both the flower pot—in the plant world—and the barracuda enclosure—in the animal world—suggest restrictions which may be interpreted variously as spiritual and physical on the human level. Gustavo spreads his roots in his beloved Playa Rosada and plants his seed, his future child, which will be nurtured with the sun and rain of his love, as he says, hoping that the future plant (a "ceiba"?) will prosper in a propitious atmosphere.

Another important symbol is Playa Rosada, reiterated again and again as Gustavo's paradise lost and found, where, according to the "sorcerer" Simón Cortijo, his protective spirit dwells. There is symbolism also in the name given the orphan friend of Gustavo, Juan Pitirre, who burns the huge trawls of commercial exploitation to protect the breeding grounds. The pitirre is "a small bird of ours that defends always victoriously its nest from the guaraguao, a large bird of prey. 'Every guaraguao has its pitirre' is an island expression."[6] Laguerre's use of the name here may also be considered a tribute to the great bard José de Diego (1866–1918), whose posthumous book of poems, *Cantos de Pitirre* [Songs of Pitirre], was published in 1950, four years before *The Ceiba Tree in the Flower Pot* was completed.

Metaphors of nature abound in the novel, in contrast to the atmosphere of New York taken over by machines, with the moon reduced to a mere street light with the Times building as its post. Gustavo compares himself to "the neurotic bird that could not eat a snail" (547) and to a chameleon who changes its appearance and keeps a watchful eye open. Human rats and ants inhabit New York. The quest for the extinct dodo by one of Javier Aguirre's guests is associated with scorn for the ordinary island fowl supplanted by attraction for the foreign and exotic. Of his wife, Clotilde, who drew him into activism, Gustavo says that she is "one of those women rivers who carry men to the waterfalls" (525). Contrasting with the ceiba of the title, hardy trees flourishing in their natural state have a special attraction for Gustavo, the two huge *quenepos* of Río Loco, the towering giant ceiba growing twenty-five meters high in Ponce, the brilliant *flamboyán* he recalls from his childhood, and an old oak tree that graces his patio at the end of the novel. Accepting his humble origin he finds his mother's affection "like the refreshing shadow of a thick-topped tree" (613).

Mythical metaphor is seen in the story of the *Imbunche* told to Gustavo by his doctor in the sanatorium. The *Imbunche* is a witch that the Araucan Indians of Chile believe robs children and carries them to a cave to change them into monsters. There are also allusions to fables (the two goats who try to cross a narrow bridge, which for Gustavo is the world) and legends of the pirates who operated on Puerto Rico's shores.

Some critics consider *The Ceiba Tree in the Flower Pot* Laguerre's finest novel for its psychological penetration and the richness of its symbolism.[7] In my opinion the strongest chapters are toward the end, centering about the barracuda episode. The first-person portrait of Gustavo Vargas has great psychological depth, as Zayas Micheli's character analysis proves; however, secondary characters are for the most part barely delineated and often nameless. It is not until the last two chapters that there is a real attempt at characterization of secondary characters, in Juan Lorenzi and Julio Antonio Cruzado. Perhaps this can be justified in that before Gustavo's final return to Pueblo people were not really important to him, for he had not learned to cherish others. In any case, the narrative prior to these chapters tends to be schematic, with abrupt transitions, and the whole book is about half the length of most of Laguerre's novels. For this critic the novel's greatest artistic achievements are to be found in the later chapters, with the surprise reappearance of characters encountered earlier in the book, the superb characterization of Lorenzi and Julio Antonio, and the barracuda episode serving as a metaphorical reprise.

The Labyrinth

The protagonist of *The Labyrinth* is Porfirio Uribe who plans to return to Puerto Rico, his law-school diploma in hand, when he unwittingly witnesses the murder of Adrián Martín, a "Santiagan" journalist, on the dark stairs of his New York boarding house and is detained for questioning. Interspersed in the generally linear narrative are recollections of the past, his twelve years in New York and before that his youth in Coamo, where as an orphaned son of circus performers—his father Mexican, his mother "Santiagan"—he was raised by his godparents, Estéfano and Catalina. His godfather had killed Catalina in a jealous rage, and with the man's imprisonment and subsequent death, Porfirio was again alone. On the ship to New York he had been befriended by Alfredo Laza, an exiled Puerto Rican Nationalist, who helped him a good deal. Extreme poverty at first led Porfirio to a life of vice from which he extricated himself working in the Dead Letter Section of the Post Office and studying law. His dreams of returning to Coamo to marry, affiliate with the majority party, and live happily ever after are interrupted by the murder of Adrián Martín. Laza and his friends, the racketeer Luis Pororico and the ex-playboy Juan Lorenzi, try to find the culprits without success, but Porfirio is cleared to return to Puerto Rico.

Porfirio's ship is sunk by a German submarine but he is rescued, and in a Virginia hospital is befriended by two Santiagan diplomats who invite him to their country, where there are more opportunities. Porfirio soon feels the charged atmosphere of the Santiagan Republic with its power struggles manipulated by his friend Dr. Jaramillo and by Leader Augusto at the top. His other friend, Jacinto Brache, reveals that he had aided Dr. Jaramillo in the murder of Adrián Martín, alias Niño Valverde, the son of a once highly esteemed public figure, Don Joaquín Valverde, who had unknowingly encouraged the elimination of Leader Augusto's enemy, author of inflammatory articles in the foreign press. Jacinto also informs Porfirio that they had brought him to the Republic as a precaution, since he had been the only witness to the assassination. Porfirio rises professionally, but in this atmosphere of tension, "suicides," and "accidents" he feels himself undergoing a terrible mutation. Jacinto Brache breaks under the pressure and while attempting to assassinate Leader Augusto, is cut down. The treacherous Dr. Jaramillo's rise to power as Augusto's trusted counselor seems assured but he is imprisoned. Juan Lorenzi, who enjoys the confidence of Leader Augusto because of their common interest in automobiles and horses, has finally been convinced by Alfredo Laza to participate in an assassination attempt for which they enlist Porfirio's help. Uribe joins operation Hunt-Down with another agent, Purificación López, and the "loyal" military man Sebastián Brache, brother of Jacinto, who pretend to bring the "prisoner" Porfirio Uribe before Leader Augusto in order to kill the tyrant at close range. A guard who recognizes Purificación warns the Leader and the conspirators are killed.

The novel may be considered in some respects a sequel to *The Ceiba Tree in the Flower Pot* with the reappearance of Juan Lorenzi, the staunch individualist who refused to compromise his personal freedom in political causes, now committed to eradicating tyranny in the Santiagan Republic (fictional name for the Dominican Republic) and, as always, escaping death, since he is on the *Barricuda* when Porfirio is killed. All the characters, both major and minor, are fully developed. The third-person narrative facilitates the presentation of a wide spectrum of scenes which otherwise could not be reasonably reproduced as the personal experience of Uribe if he were exclusive narrator. The narrative does, however, incorporate his feelings and point of view indirectly. Surprises and recognitions heighten interest in the plot intrigue, as when Porfirio learns the identity of his Santiagan "friends" and that of Adrián Martín.

As a protagonist Uribe resembles other Laguerrean characters in that he is an orphan, suffers loneliness, and struggles with conflicting values. The novel is atypical in the almost complete absence of landscape, as J. Beauchamp observes, for descriptions of nature appear only in the protagonist's recollections of Puerto Rico or in ironic contrast to the monstrosity of Leader Augusto, who "overshadowed nature itself" (184).[8]

Greek mythology provides the major symbolical elements of the novel, which are underscored by the author. The title refers to the labyrinth which King Minos of Crete ordered Daedalus to construct in order to house the Minotaur, fierce monster, half man and half bull, which devoured human tribute exacted from the Athenians. As Bulfinch tells us, "Theuseus resolved to deliver his countrymen from this calamity, or to die in the attempt."[9] Ariadne, daughter of King Minos, gave Theseus a sword and a clew of thread to kill the monster and find his way out of the labyrinth. There are clearly several labyrinths in the novel. That of New York imprisions Porfirio in solitude, prejudice, and poverty; education seems to be the Ariadne's thread which will liberate him at last. There is also Uribe's interior labyrinth in which he struggles to free himself from the "tyranny of everyday necessities," with the hope of material advancement, but his final escape lies in lending his support to an act of supreme spiritual value, coinciding with the escape from "the worst labyrinth of all," the Santiagan Republic. Observing the beautiful tropical landscape, Uribe says, "it was unthinkable that a monster was running loose in this paradise" (119). Two old and powerful families had created the monster and now could not control it. The episode in which a heifer escapes from its halter and charges the august Leader reminds us of the original Minotaur's taurine component.

Another myth appearing in the novel is reference to Dr. Jaramillo as Bellerophon hunting down the Chimera (the head of the rival family, Don Joaquín Valverde), falling from the antechamber of Olympus (Leader Augusto's favor). The Orpheus myth is also important, both explicitly and implicitly. Jacinto Brache metaphorically calls himself Orpheus and his fiancée, Hortensia, Eurydice, referring to the master musician who attempted to rescue his wife from the Underworld of Hades, but looked back and lost her. The Santiagan violinist is rendered useless in a mission deliberately ordered by Leader Augusto in which he loses a finger and he is reduced to conducting the "Orpheus Orchestra" at the monster's bidding in the Santiagan Hades. Music in fact becomes a major motif in the novel, with reference to Porfirio's *bombardino,* the baritone horn bequeathed to him by his godfather. Porfirio treats the broken horn as a person; it becomes his companion during his twelve years in New York, associated with the sobs of Estéfano and his own tragic feelings. It also represents Puerto Rico, for the baritone horn is an essential part of the *danza* music of the island. Other "instruments" join what might be called Porfirio's own "Orpheus Orchestra" in the metropolitan Hades, the wailing of foghorns and the sounds of his heart throbbing "its two organ notes" (14).

The *bombardino,* whose lament is inextricably linked to Porfirio's past in Coamo and his life as a "dead letter" in New York, is sunk with the ship, with a liberating effect:

Hadn't he felt as though a whole life had been sunk when the *bombardino* was engulfed by the sea? He had even imagined that as the ship began to sink, the abandoned instrument had begged to be rescued in its deep, broken voice. . . . When we are isolated for years on end, we become more conscious of the objects which accompany us. He had let the sorrowful old soul of the poor *bombardino* influence him! (122)

He feels reborn as he embarks upon a new era in his life but from that time on he is an Orpheus without an instrument in a new Hades, joining Jacinto Brache, and at the end taking part in a similar feat to save the Eurydice of freedom from the monster of the netherworld.

The first part of the novel is dedicated to Porfirio's experience as the wandering Puerto Rican in New York in the 1940s. His experience there is more traumatic, perhaps, than that of Gustavo Vargas of *The Ceiba Tree in the Flower Pot* in that it is prolonged. He is the victim of disparaging epithets, prejudice, indifference, and loneliness. As a Puerto Rican he is considered an immediate suspect when a crime is committed and he is scorned by unfeeling, robotlike police. Even superiors and teachers who know him well are not beyond suspecting that a Puerto Rican might be capable of doing anything. Porfirio describes the collective boredom of the city on a typical Saturday, the mouths of immigrants as open wounds, and their lives as "uprooted plants," echoing the metaphor of *The Ceiba Tree in the Flower Pot.* An interesting negative aspect of the Puerto Rican immigration, becoming more and more "comfortable" in the new environment, is embodied in Luis Pororico (his name a distortion of "Porto Rico"), in charge of his own "territory" of organized rackets. Laguerre's view of the city includes some humor, as in the incident in which Uribe, impressed with the "courtesy" of a subway passenger who vacates his seat for him, has not realized that he was taken for a bum to be avoided.

The second part of the novel represents Laguerre's contribution to the fictional treatment of a major Hispanic theme, that of the tyrant. Literary predecessors in Latin America include Domingo Faustino Sarmiento's *Facundo* (1847), José Mármol's *Amalia* (1851), and Miguel Ángel Asturias's *Señor Presidente* (1946). Two Spanish novels treating Latin American dictatorships, preceded by Valle-Inclán's *Tirano Banderas* (1926), appeared almost at the same time as *The Labyrinth*, Francisco Ayala's *Muertes de perro* [Dogs' Death], published the year before, in 1958, and E. F. Granell's *La novela del Indio Tupinamba* [The Novel of the Indian Tupinamba], in 1959. The latter includes a Surrealist portrayal of the Trujillo era in the Dominican Republic. Laguerre's approach to the theme is realistic and incorporates the perspective of his protagonist as an involved observer.

Laguerre's obvious admiration for the conspirators in their struggle against tyranny deserves some comment in view of his rather consistent stand against violence as a way of dealing with problems in Puerto Rico. It is significant that Juan Lorenzi, who in *The Ceiba Tree in the Flower Pot* would not use his passion for freedom to serve the Nationalist cause in Puerto Rico, now lends his support to hunting down Leader Augusto in the neighboring republic.

The novel was undoubtedly inspired by historical events which occurred in the preceding years, notably the assassination of two well-known writers. The *New York Times* of October 4, 1952, carried the following report about the first case:

> The victim's background of opposition to the Trujillo regime in the Dominican Republic imparted mystery yesterday to the slaying of Andres Requena, 44 years old, of 601 West 110th Street. Mr. Requena was a former diplomatic or consular employee of the Dominican Republic, a former Army private first class, and the co-publisher of a pamphlet that periodically attacked the Trujillo Administration.
>
> He was killed shortly before midnight Thursday in the ground-floor hallway of a tenement at 243 Madison Street, on the Lower East Side near Clinton Street. Mr. Requena went there by taxi—the neighborhood was unfamiliar to him. (p. 3, col. 8)

The waiting taxi driver reported that several shots were fired and the victim fell in the dim hallway.

Laguerre's account of the slaying of Adrián (not too different from the name *Andrés*) Martín closely follows the circumstances of the assassination of Requena, author of an anti-Trujillo novel entitled *Cementerio sin cruces* [Cemetery without Crosses], as well as the aforementioned pamphlet. Additional coverage of the incident in the *Times* on October 4 and 5 spoke of threats received by the victim, Dominican attempts to exonerate Trujillo from any responsibility, and accusations by Dominican exiles in Havana attributing the slaying to the tyranny of the Trujillo regime.

Another such incident took place in 1956, with the "disappearance" of Jesús de Galíndez as he entered a subway station in New York City. Galíndez was a Spanish exile who accepted political asylum in Santo Domingo in 1939, where he taught in the country's diplomatic school and was active in the Department of Labor and National Economy. He displeased Trujillo by arbitrating several strikes favorably for the workers, and, fearing harassment, he left for the United States in 1946. He settled in New York, where he wrote articles for Spanish newspapers and periodicals in the United States and Latin America. Shortly after Columbia University approved his doctoral dissertation, entitled "The Era of Trujillo," an exposé of the regime, Galíndez, who taught at the university, was driven by a student to a subway entrance to go on by underground to his apartment on lower Fifth Avenue. After that no one ever saw him again and his body was never found. The widely publicized kidnapping and presumed murder became an international cause célèbre, complicated further by the death in the Dominican Republic the following year of a young aviator from Oregon, Gerald Lester Murphy, copilot in a Trujillo-owned Dominican airline, which was assumed related to the disappearance of Galíndez.[10]

The Adrián Martín murder in *The Labyrinth* is obviously a fictional crime patterned after these incidents, but Laguerre situates his story during World War II, a period when the anti-Trujillo activities of Dominican exiles were intensified. The assassination attempt in which Porfirio Uribe is killed would thus coincide with two unsuccessful invasions of the Dominican Republic at Cayo Confites and Luperón in 1947 and 1949, respectively, by conspirators.

While *The Labyrinth* is not a historical novel in the strict sense, it does represent indirectly Laguerre's comment on the Trujillo regime and the Requena and Galíndez affairs. In fact, some of the proper names in the novel seem to echo prominent names associated with Trujillo. Don *Joaquín Val*verde, for example, suggests the name of Trujillo's Secretary of Foreign Relations, a figurehead who heaped praise on the Generalísimo, *Joaquín Bal*aguer (the *v* and *b* are pronounced similarly in Spanish). *Porfirio Uribe*'s name seems like a shortened and transposed version of *Porfirio Rubi*rosa, the playboy diplomat and first husband of Trujillo's eldest daughter, Flor. Although Laguerre's protagonist shares Rubirosa's love for "the good life" and is favored by the Leader, the similarity of names becomes ironic in view of Uribe's low-keyed personality and final commitment to self-sacrifice. The surname Jaram*illo,* ending in the same way as Truj*illo,* reminds us of the character's aspirations to power, which would only prove that there would be little difference between a Trujillo and a Jaramillo, or one heartless dictator and another. A few other similarities crop up, too, like Augusto and Sebastián, denoting two different characters, for Trujillo's Secret Police Chief was Augusto Sebastián, a Spanish exile.[11] In view of the sometimes surprising nature of reality and prophetic character of art (which the Surrealists accept quite naturally), we offer the following coincidence: two years after the publication of *The Labyrinth,* portraying the foiled conspiracy masterminded by *A*lfredo L*aza,* Trujillo was in fact assassinated by a group of conspirators, among them the "active and efficient" *A*ntonio de la M*aza!*[12]

Laguerre employs linguistic and situational irony to reproduce the atmosphere of repression rather than resorting to detailed descriptions of atrocities, which his sensitivity rejects. The worst case is that of the beauty queen Paulina, forcibly seduced by the Leader, whose baby is delivered by her husband, Dr. Jaramillo, who kills it. It is one example of how Leader Augusto destroys lives and breeds a series of malignant acts. In general Laguerre reflects the tension pervading life in the Republic, with particular sadness for the effects on the university and young people. We perceive the collective schizophrenia that exists in the Santiagan Republic, where people are afraid to talk and even more afraid to listen. There is black humor in the episode in the public car when an innocent comment about the condition of the roads is interpreted as criticism of the "great benefactor," making it difficult to find conversation which cannot be construed as treason. There are constant allusions to mystery, reticence, "suicides," and "accidents."

Besides the ubiquitous portrait of Leader Augusto, there are personal views of him as a master politician, pitting family against family, dividing family loyalties, and accepting the fawning praise of his advisors while planning their fate. Augusto dines on dove and despite his imposing uniform, covered with medals, is described by Jacinto Brache as "nothing more than a man whose life is contained in his digestive tube" (198). For Colonel Sebastián Brache the tyrant is simply "a man in a hurry to empty his bowels" (268). Emphasis on these primary bodily functions underscores his animalistic nature.

Laguerre's principal technique is irony, describing the "glorious statesman" as "the Father of their Country," who receives recognition "of his many merits and his tireless efforts in behalf of the Fatherland" (234). "What other illustrious chief of state, no matter how glorious he might be, could compare his deeds with those of Leader Augusto?" (236). In truth such hyperbolic epithets abounded in singing Trujillo's praises and were not viewed with any irony at all! The Republic itself is described with great irony: "The Leader's private secretary and counselor was Jacinto Martínez, a man who had fled from 'the bloody dictatorship' in Spain to enjoy the benefits of the excellent democracy presided over by Leader Augusto" (138). The contrast with Puerto Rico is also treated ironically. Jaramillo says of his return to the Republic after being born in Puerto Rico: "I wanted to live in a free country, apparently even when I was a baby" although the true irony is not apparent until later in the book (107). When his two Santiagan "friends" invite him to accompany them to the Republic, Uribe decides "that it wouldn't be a bad idea to try his luck in a country with many more opportunities than Puerto Rico" (110). Don Joaquín, himself a victim of the tyrant, tells Porfirio, "you have a future here. In your country there are too many people for too little land. I don't know if it's true, but they tell me there are few opportunities in Puerto Rico for young men like you" (186). As it turns out, the Santiagan Republic is not exactly the land of opportunity.

Other ironies also appear in the novel, such as the sign on the sanatorium for the mad: WE OWE EVERYTHING TO LEADER AUGUSTO, which is unfortunately true, although Augusto disclaims responsibility for Jacinto Brache's problem "since no one is responsible for another man's madness (236). Oddly enough, in *The Era of Trujillo* Jesús de Galíndez relates that "sometimes sycophancy becomes accidentally bitter irony as, for example in the sign at the entrance of the insane asylum at Nigua: *Todo se lo debemos a Trujillo"* [We owe everything to Trujillo]"![13]

The Labyrinth, at least in the second part, is not a novel about Puerto Rico but rather about Puerto Ricans risking their lives with a sense of Antillean unity like that espoused by Eugenio María de Hostos. Perhaps, too, it presents an example for Puerto Rico, an example to be avoided, of dictatorship and tyranny. It may be argued that Uribe is not really a hero since he merely accedes to Lorenzi's proposals with the idea of living in the memory of others. Regardless of his motives, the fact is that he had lived almost thirty-three years, the age of Christ at his crucifixion, without having executed a great act of generosity and sacrifice until that moment which leads him out of his multiple labyrinths. The words written on the paper found on Laza's body provide the final comment: "No one can kill us. Tyrant, be sure of it, we will return, our numbers multiplied, and in a thousand voices we will demand justice and freedom. For the world was not conceived by a monster" (275). There is tremendous irony in Leader Augusto's order, "Kill those corpses," for it is not only impossible in the physical realm but also in that of collective memory which eventually resulted in a successful termination of a personalist regime that lasted thirty-one years. Like the Puerto Ricans in his novel Laguerre showed he cared about the neighboring republic and its fight against the Minotaur in *The Labyrinth.*

Chapter Seven
Who Am I? The Problem of Identity

Cauce sin río [River Bed without a River], published in 1962, and *El fuego y su aire* [Fire and Its Air], which followed eight years later, pose questions of individual identity while at the same time suggesting that the problem is also a collective one in Puerto Rico. The protagonist of the earlier novel flees from a frivolous urban environment to find himself and his values; in the second novel the protagonist searches for keys to his unknown past and in the process learns about the many ways of being—or not being—a Puerto Rican. Both are fraught with contradictions which must be resolved before they can feel free, and in these novels criticism is directed agianst the "fictitious" life of well-to-do families in San Juan.

Despite the similarities implicit in the common quest for identity and authenticity, Laguerre writes two quite different novels. Self-realization takes different turns in each novel, with nature as the positive alternative in the first and history in the second, where identity becomes inextricably linked to the protagonist's destiny. The novels are also divergent in form, technique, point of view (concentrated in one, diffusive in the other), and tone. It is not difficult to perceive increased pessimism in the later book, in which the same conditions of vanity and frivolity continue to exist, combined with other problems in a political, commercial, and moral atmosphere which the author evidently decries, without the alternative of returning to a more salubrious life in the country.

River Bed without a River

In the first half of the novel, protagonist and narrator Víctor Hugo Rodríguez Sandeau sees a drop of blood while shaving and recounts his fear of dying from leukemia like his father. The experience provokes a crisis of conscience in which he realizes the emptiness of his dedication to affluence and material possessions and resolves to return to his childhood country home, Sanetién. Narrative, recall, and introspection combine to portray his life as an eminently successful builder who knew how to take advantage of flourishing tourism and industrialization, who lives in a prestigious development called Green Plains and serves on several of the governor's commissions. He suddenly feels the weight of his "useless passion for accumulating objects" (16) and of his wife and daughter's constant involvement with society affairs and personal vanities.[1] With compunction for his previous indifference he tries to help a neighbor, Juan Arenas, retrieve the position from which he had been unjustly dismissed, but meets with the opposition of his influential friends, among them Justo Plaza, a boyhood companion. Víctor's past is also a part of his present anxieties: his desertion of friends involved in the 1948 Nationalist protests in the university; his unsuccessful marriage to Susie, who subsequently married his boyhood friend Alfonso II San Román, now a physician; and his own later marriage to the latter's old girl friend Marina. He also remembers Merche, who took care of him when he was little and disappeared from the house when he was six, and the cries of pain of his father, who suffered from cancer. Víctor receives a visit from another old friend, María Dolores or Marilola, whose conversation helps him realize even further the emptiness of his marriage and the need for change. He shows Marilola a letter from a José Sandó, who claims to be his half-brother and demands property rights. After a frustrated suicide attempt, Víctor announces his decision to go to Sanetién to rest, in the hope of recovering his values and filling his "river bed without a river."

The second half of the novel finds Víctor "ready, like a seed, to take root in the land," occupying the family home near Río Loco, the river whose channel has been deviated in an irrigation project. He makes friends with his brother, whose mother is Merche, and now realizes why she had left years before. Víctor becomes attached to his nephews and finds himself falling in love with the nurse who comes to give him his injections, Carmen Eugenia or Carmencho, whom he recalls from his youth and who, as it turns out, had always liked him. She is unhappily married to a bitter and jealous man, Lijuán, another of Víctor's early playmates. He had been involved in unsavory ventures in New York and had been blinded by a gunshot wound, after which he met and married his nurse Carmencho. Lijuán tries to shoot Víctor but José warns his brother in time. The man's later suicide before the prospect of being arrested on a warrant from New York frees Carmencho, but Marina will not divorce Víctor, who has found peace and happiness in Carmencho's company and that of his brother's family in the natural setting of Sanetién. A letter from Carmencho, who has left to do social work abroad, assures him of her undying love and urges him to live in accordance with his conscience now that he has found himself with the help of her love. Like the Río Loco whose river bed fills with the rain from the mountains, Víctor is ready to accept the flow of life in the country, free from the vanities of Green Plains.

Laguerre himself provides us with the suggestion of a very graphic parallel to the structure of his novel in *Pulso de Puerto Rico* [Pulse of Puerto Rico], where he twice refers to El Greco's famous painting *The Burial of Count Orgaz,* first in discussion of dual themes in an Epistle of the poet De Diego Padró and then to compare the three planes usually found in Francisco Arriví's theater corresponding to worldly, spiritual, and "tangential" aspects of the painting.[2] El Greco divides the pictorial space into two major sections, heaven and earth, with serious men in black as observers of the pompous burial and the ascension of the count's soul into heaven. In similar fashion *River Bed without a River* is divided into two balanced parts of seven chapters apiece which portray first the "living death" of Víctor in Green Plains and then his spiritual rebirth in Sanetién. The tangential observers are the readers, into whose own world the characters intrude, for Laguerre dedicates the novel to his daughter Beatriz María and to Carmen Eugenia (his fictional character), "who live beyond all transience," and the protagonist Víctor comes forward to furnish the epigraph: "I object to civilization's putting its foot where it ought to put its soul." Other "tangential" elements are characters and places which reappear from other Laguerre novels, particularly *The Ceiba Tree in the Flower Pot,* extending the ambience of one novel into his greater fictional world that represents Puerto Rico. Indeed, *The Burial of Count Orgaz,* a painting that obviously interests Laguerre, may provide a surprising number of insights into *River Bed without a River,* for just as a young boy is present in the pictorial scene,

José Sandó's boys grace the world of Sanetién, and the novel, like the picture, is the story of its protagonist's spritual salvation.

Each of the two divisions of *River Bed without a River* can almost be read independently, since the first ends with Víctor's optimism about finding himself in Sanetién and the second recapitulates many events of the first. The protagonist's retrospection does not follow chronological sequence, as is true in real-life meditation, and as events treated previously reappear, new details and explanations are added, giving the reader the impression that the novel is being written as it progresses. The flow of events is consequential, proceeding from the protagonist's experience. If occasionally something appears unlikely, such as Víctor's receiving a letter his wife had written to her old suitor and neighbor, Dr. San Román, the reader's possible protest of inverisimilitude is cleverly anticipated with the protagonist himself offering the comment that "in truth, it seems incredible" (144). As for the sight of blood before the mirror as impulse for an almost immediate transformation in Víctor's way of thinking, it is not the least bit incredible in view of the psychological impact the perspective of death may exert and also the literary precedent in José de Espronceda's great poem *El diablo mundo* [The Devil's World, 1840], in which the poet's contemplation of his image in the mirror while shaving occasions a traumatic discovery of the fleeting nature of time. Another effective technique is the alternation between past tense and present in the narration, with the latter corresponding frequently to events and descriptions which are pleasant. The beauties of nature are communicated by lyrical passages that appeal to all the senses.

As we have noted, the first part of the novel corresponds to the worldly plane of El Greco's painting, and in this context it is interesting to note the subtle usage of terminology associated with death and religion which makes it clear that Víctor's life in Green Plains is a form of living death. Previously called *Los Robles* ("The Oaks"), the name Green Plains, given in English, besides suggesting imitation of United States standards, foreign to the native spirit, seems like an appropriate designation for a cemetery in which the mighty oaks of yesteryear have given way to luxurious homes that function as mausoleums for its inhabitants, who refuse to abandon their worldly flesh. Mariola refers to her cousin San Román as a "corpse" and "an ulcer with a white, bloodless epidermis" (59) and Víctor describes him as "neatly dressed, with the neatness of a cadaver who has just been prepared to be placed in the box" (35). Contemplating his existence in Green Plains, Víctor recognizes: "Here I am, among a bunch of abandoned things, submitted to the domination of objects, in the middle of a cemetery populated by specters" (26). His wife reacts as though she had been kissed by a corpse, he tells us. At the end of the first part of the novel Víctor awakens from a significant nightmare in which he feels himself enclosed in a coffin, undoubtedly a reflection of his living death in the "cemetery" of Green Plains. The metaphor may be further extended to the island in general, which Mariola calls a country of "absent people" referring to those who have emigrated en masse. Víctor feels that uncontrolled industrialization and construction will lead to ruin, leaving the island for the vultures (71). He sees Marilola's visit as an "unexpected resurrection" from the "semideath" of absence (51). In their childhood days in San Germán, however, a coffin was simply a place to steal a kiss in Marilola's uncle's funerary establishment or to punish a companion like Justito Plaza for playing a cruel trick on a friend.

Religious allusions are just abundant enough to be noticeable in a careful reading and serve as ironic commentary to the false cult of materialism in Green Plains, where social debuts are the rites of "this religion of frivolities" to which Víctor has bestowed "adoration" for over ten years (26). Víctor refers to his father's "transfiguration" in closeness to nature, to Juan Arenas as "a medieval excommunicant" (79), and to Marilola's visit as "a miracle." He speaks to her as "one submits to a confessor" (67) in a conversation between "two ghosts" and notes her singing her own requiem. It may also be significant that she has just returned from doing social work in Pátzcuaro and the Island of Janitzio in Mexico, places well known for their rather bizarre processions to the cemeteries on All Saints Day ("the Day of the Dead" in Spanish) to leave food for the dead. There is also a contrast between the "Carnival" of Green Plains, represented so graphically in the ridiculous French imperial farce enacted in the coronation of Víctor's daughter as a beauty queen, and the equally grotesque superficial observance of Lent by the women, interested only in appearances.

Additional irony is present in the proliferation of "saints" in proper names and geographic designations: *San* Germán and *San* Juan, *Sane*-tién (adaption of Saint-Etienne in France, place of origin of Víctor's mother's family), Dr. *San* Román, Víctor *San*deau, and José *San*dó. Víctor calls himself a "proselyte" of easy wealth and frivolity and his friends (and real Pharisees) from the capital who visit him in Sanetién call upon the "Pharisee" to help them"preach from house to house" their programs (140). He is a mistaken saint, proselyte of the inauthentic "saintliness" accorded to money (his name phonetically suggests "dough," the colloquial term for money in English), but in the unperverted world of Sanetién he finds spiritual salvation. He tells Carmencho, whose love has filled his channel, "You gave me back life after I journeyed, discouraged, through emptiness" (180).

Biblical allusions are also present, as in Víctor's recollection of Job's lament, "Why was I not hidden from view as an untimely birth, as infants that have never seen the light?" (18).[3] In ironic contrast to the biblical Job, bereft of the material blessings formerly bestowed upon him, Víctor finds himself anguuished by an excess of wealth, respect, and success unaccompanied by moral satisfaction. His childhood incursions into the garden of Justito's awe-inspiring aunts to steal cherries may be interpreted as a variation of the Garden of Eden.

It is significant and ironic that Víctor's fears of cancer precipitate his transformation and regeneration, removing him precisely from the spiritual death which has afflicted him for many years. We suspect that Laguerre believes the worst cancer is spiritual and is already present in those whose lives are similar to many residents of Green Plains. This would seem confirmed by the metaphorical use of cancer when Marilola comments upon her disillusion with social reform she witnessed in Mexico: "they want to cure the cancer with narcotics" (173). Material possessions are the narcotics used in Green Plains to treat the cancer of emptiness. The red blood which frightens Víctor is not the anemic blood of leukemia and it serves as a stimulus for life. Imagining what might have been his future in a neurological clinic if he had continued in the "whirlpool of specters," he exclaims, "It would be better to have inherited the illness of my father" (118), the physical cancer, rather than a moral cancer that devours the spirit. His final victory is at the end of the novel when he is called upon to continue even without the presence of the woman he loves, secure in the knowledge that he is loved and in the company of his "true" family.

A significant indication of the protagonist's problem in finding his authentic identity in the representation and farce of Green Plains is the Cervantine technique of name variation. Sandeau continues to use the original French form of his surname while in contrast his half-brother Sandó's Spanish adaptation, product of vigorous crossbreeding, adjusts to the culture of Puerto Rico, as does the Hispanization of Saint-Etienne to Sanetién. The name of *Víctor Hugo* Rodríguez Sandeau may be a tribute to the French author who championed social causes in his novel *Les Miserables,* whose centenary of publication was precisely the same year *River Bed without a River* was published. The contrasts between Green Plains and Sanetién are further revealed in the name forms used in each place. As expressions of endearment and affection in Sanetién, Víctor is called Virrucho by his mother and Merche, and Vitón by his nephew and namesake, called Vitín. There too his brother is Joseíto; Mercedes, Merche; and Carmen Eugenia, Carmencho. In Green Plains Víctor is diversely referred to as H. R. in business and by his own daughter, and Víctor by his wife. The women's names, Marina and Maritza, remain unaltered in the general absence of intimacy and affection.

It would be superfluous to relate here all the numerous examples of the symbolism proceeding from the title since Laguerre makes it perfectly clear to the reader that both Víctor Sandeau and Green Plains are river beds without rivers and that in the natural setting of Sanetién, Víctor's empty channel is filled with love and family values just as the channel of Río Loco is filled by the life-giving rains. He recognizes, however, that the river's waters no longer flow to the lagoon where as a child he delighted in swimming, but have been diverted for irrigation in order to benefit the common good. So too will he adjust his priorities from private satisfaction to consideration of others. The title of the novel functions as a symbol, but also as a lyrical leitmotif which reappears throughout in moments of spiritual uplifting. There are also minor symbols like the clock without hands (suggesting eternity), the dog *Buendía* (collective unconsciousness), and the rocking chair (parents and the past), all appearing in Sanetién.

As in the case of symbols, ideas are not hidden but rather presented before the reader with honest straightforwardness, particularly toward the end, as in *The Ceiba Tree in the Flower Pot:* the importance of education, the defense of Puerto Rican traditions balanced with the support of progress in harmony with these traditions, patriotism that is not dependent upon great deeds but rather public concern, and the resolution of "interim status" in the individual and the island.

There is a clear relationship between the individual protagonist and the collective reference appearing in the subtitle of the novel, "Diary of My Generation." Luis O. Zayas Micheli situates Víctor in the generation of the 1940s in Puerto Rico unable to harmonize the nationalistic spirit of the 1930s with industrial and technocratic advances, but this is somewhat perplexing since Laguerre specifically calls the novel a diary of his own generation and he is associated unanimously with that of the 1930s.[4] Since Víctor Sandeau was thirty-six years old during the university disturbances of 1948, he would be only six years younger than the author, which by Ortega y Gasset's formula would place them in the same generation. Conceding some overlap between the 1930s and 1940s, this would be a generation of transition. At the same time the term "generation" in the novel does not seem to represent a blanket condemnation, but rather refers to those who have succumbed to artificial values of success, prestige, and possessions, creating an island within the island. There are, however, signs of regeneration even in the metropolitan area's cult of power and wealth, for Víctor's first wife, Susie, rediscovers her Puerto Rican heritage and he accepts being the first "casualty" of his "generation" in order to find himself.

In keeping with the collective perspective, Laguerre uses the symbol of the *cemí*. The *cemíes* were minor gods carved in stone by the pre-Colombian Taíno Indians of Puerto Rico, who revered nature. Their closeness to the individual and the family was implicit in their images, worn around the neck or placed in the home.[5] In Sanetién Víctor feels his "sleeping *cemí*" begin to awaken, and laments "not having listened before to the voice of the *cemí* that I carry in my spirit" (189). Víctor Sandeau provides an example of Laguerre's faith in the reawakening of the historical conscience, even in the wasteland of places like Green Plains.

Fire and Its Air

The novel begins when Pedro Jose Expósito (whose surname means "orphan"), almost twenty, is about to leave the home for mentally retarded children where he was brought as a traumatized, silent eight-year-old. He has been offered a scholarship to study music because of his exceptional ability in that field, but is unable to dedicate himself to his studies, troubled about the mysteries of his unknown past, only recalled in fragments: the words "Puerto Rico," vague images of the sea, and a nightmarish vision of two pairs of legs near a bed, a woman's scream, and a pool of blood on the floor. He considers becoming a priest but goes to live with a young woman he meets, Ruth, a survivor of the Holocaust, whom he would like to marry and take to Puerto Rico, but she turns him down. Pedro and his Dominican friend Ulises, a staunch anti-Trujillo patriot, are drafted and in Korea fight with the Puerto Rican brigade. Afterwards the friends join the Merchant Marine on the ship *Prometeo* ("Prometheus"), commanded by the mysterious Captain Sanrug. Pedro has many conversations with Adalberto Linares, a professor of social studies in Puerto Rico, who paints a pessimistic picture of the island, in contrast to Pedro's idealist image gleaned from posters in the tourist office and readings in the public library. Also on board the *Prometeo* are Javier Aguirre, the vice-governor of Puerto Rico, and Oscar Martín, ex-Nationalist turned "American" who with the flick of an accent conveniently becomes Oscar *Mar*tin. When Ulises discovers Captain Sanrug's dealings in drugs, he is in danger of being denounced to Immigration as a Communist (ironic in view of the medals for valor won in Korea), so he jumps overboard and is found by some fishermen who take him to Puerto Rico. Sanrug and Martín testify against him and he is deported right into the arms of the tyrant Trujillo.

In Puerto Rico Pedro finds that Adalberto's description of the moral climate is exact. As a nurses' aid in a hospital he becomes fast friends with Lori Taveras, a victim of multiple sclerosis, whose father, Don Lorenzo, is a cookie tycoon. Lori's best friend is Elda Astol, Adalberto Linares's sweetheart. With Lori's death, the arrest of her brother Larry (together with Captain Sanrug) on drug charges, and betrayal by his business associates, Don Lorenzo's conscience as a father and a Puerto Rican awakens. His vane wife, María Luisa, tries to attract the man she had intended to be Lori's husband, Oscar Martín, son of the man she had loved. During this time Pedro has progressed as pianist and arranger at the Caribe Hotel. With information provided by María Luisa Taveras, Pedro begins to realize that he is the son of her old lover Don Carlos Martín, and in La Parguera and Puerto Real he learns from some old fishermen the details of how his father had killed his mother, the mestiza Jesusa Cerame, and the circumstances which had brought him to New York in a traumatized condition.

Adalberto, Elda, a repentant María Luisa, and Don Lorenzo try to locate Pedro, who disappeared after debating between becoming a maverick priest or a hero. Among the names of Puerto Ricans taking part in an invasion against the tyrant in the Dominican Republic which appear in the newspaper, Adalberto sees that of "Pedro Cerame." The mystery of his possible survival ends the novel just as that of his past began it.[6] The theme of identity yields to that of destiny.[7]

Critics have observed that *Fire and Its Air* is one of Laguerre's most complex novels technically and ideologically.[8] There is generous use of interior monologue and according to Zayas Micheli, the chaotic structure reflects a chaotic world. Nevertheless, this impression of confusion is not generalized in the novel but rather characteristic of the first chapters in harmony with the psychic confusion of Pedro José Expósito. This impression is dissipated as the novel progresses and the narration becomes more linear, with individual chapters dedicated to particular characters or situations.

It seems useful and appropriate, since Pedro is a talented musician, to explain the complexities of the novel in musical terms, which in many instances coincide with those of literary commentary. We would choose the symphony to describe Laguerre's masterful orchestration of story, language, symbol, and point of view, a symphony unified by the recurrence of certain melodic and rhythmic motives. As in a symphony, the first movement is predominant and corresponds here to Pedro José Expósito's dilemma. Other "movements" involve Ulises, Adalberto and Elda, and the Taveras family, ending in a return to the predominant theme of Pedro's identity and destiny. Melodic integration among these movements is provided by the person of Pedro, who retreats as a focal point, and by the ideas of Adalberto Linares, stated by him or recalled by other characters. As in the symphonic mode, there are digressions, fragmentations, alteration, recombination, reharmonization, and restatement or reprise.

A constant narrative technique in the novel is the sliding point of view, a sort of counterpoint in which third-person narration slides into the first person and back again, alternating with a third interwoven voice of conscience usually in italics. This is present in several main characters and not only in treatment of the protagonist. While suggesting alienation and fragmentation, particularly in the case of the latter, it has a positive connotation in that self-observation may stir the conscience and lead to change. In one outstanding example of sliding point of view Pedro "lost himself in thought, inventing stories and characters: I contemplate myself from afar as if I were another person, and I ask him what he is doing out of place" (78). [9]

A new procedure in Laguerre is the proliferation of compounded words, not to impress the reader with the verbal novelty but rather to create varied effects. Compound expressions underscore the irony of slogans like "travel-now-and-pay-later" (42), "soldiers-of-democracy" (65), or "Island-of-my-dreams" (113) used to control collective psychology. Pedro's recollection of "the-legs-around-the-bed" as one expression reminds us that memory and visual imagery present themselves as a solid block and not in the separation that verbal description imposes. Pedro's awakening from sleep is rendered appropriately by words that adhere to each other like the "sticky-sleep-that-adheres-to-his eyelids" (52).

Another relatively unusual aspect of the novel is the inversion of Laguerre's customary intrusion of fictitious characters into our real world (as in the dedication and epigraph of *River Bed without a River*) by allowing people and events from the outside world to enter his novel. World events such as the Russians' launching of *Sputnik,* the Berlin Wall—compared to the wall of prejudice in Harlem, the reign of Trujillo in the Dominican Republic—no longer disguised as the Santiagan Republic of *The Labyrinth,* the Korean War, and the "convenient" use of McCarthyism's epithet of "Communist" all appear in *Fire and Its Air.* The impression of reality is increased by the presence of well-known Puerto Rican personalities, like San Juan's famous Mayoress Doña Felisa (Rincón de Gautier), who briefly visits the Taveras home but leaves to fulfill obligations in the slums; the Spanish sculptor residing in Puerto Rico, Compostela, known for his figures of penguins mocking human attitudes; and the then governor, unnamed in the novel but absolutely identifiable in the uncomplimentary allusion to "the Man-who-went-for-a-walk-with-his-own-statue, inherited from his father, and made a religion of opulence" (165). He refers to

Luis Muñoz Marín, committed to "progress," and to his father, Luis Muñoz Rivera. Another notable case of introducing elements of outside reality into fiction is seen in the very subtle intrusion of titles of other Laguerre novels, *River Bed without a River* (259), *The Labyrinth* (276), and *The Undertow* (277). They appear simply as words almost imperceptibly woven into the text.

Narrative tone in *Fire and Its Air* is notably more sarcastic and critical than in previous novels, communicating rather ostensible disillusion and an open attack on the Establishment, social prejudice, economic exploitation, materialism, commercialism, servility, and the lack of authentic human values. Humor is abundant but barbed, as when Pedro, asked his nationality, answers, "If I am fighting for the freedom of Korea, I must be Korean" (64), and in the American "whose name in English was a bad word in Spanish" (109), Lou Hudders. Yet, despite the critical attitude that pervades the novel, Laguerre retains his characteristic charitable attitude toward individual people, no doubt agreeing with Adalberto that "there is always something incorruptibly good in the conscience of men" (272). The author generously allows Don Lorenzo and María Luisa to "touch bottom," realize their errors, and formulate new intentions for improvement. This is kept within the realm of plausibility by the persistence of some of the old habits and gestures.

Laguerre may be counted on not to let artistic virtuosity outshine content but rather to maintain it subservient to his larger purpose. He is most interested in portraying a moral climate, and the major instruments of language, structure, situation, symbol, and myth all combine to reflect that climate. It is especially interesting to observe how specific situations in the novel later assume ironic symbolic significance. What seems like a natural part of the plot extends and radiates outward and functions metaphorically. Pedro's orphanhood is a concrete situation, for example, but it soon becomes apparent that both Lori and Larry Taveras are orphaned with their parents still alive. Laguerre calls Pedro "child of a womb of shadows" (218) and describes Larry as "searching for the womb of shadows" (225). María Luisa acknowleges that she has failed Lori and Larry: "There is no worse orphanhood than that of the mother who has not known how to be a mother" (269). Finally, we realize that many of the characters in the novel are orphans of the spirit.

Similar irony may be adduced with regard to Larry's addiction to the "Artificial Paradises" of drugs which become symbolical of "an artificial world in which commercial advertising takes the place of the drugs" (224). "The traffickers of artificial paradises are child's play compared to the tragic deeds of the traffickers of consciences" (255–56). Laguerre criticizes also *"outside, in the world of politics, the politicaddicts, defectors of tradition, drugged by material successes"* (221).

Lori Taveras is paralyzed by physical illness just as others are by moral infirmity. Don Lorenzo is characterized as moving in a wheelchair of square wheels. Elda Astol's mother, who is, like Lori, confined to a wheelchair, is explicitly described as "doubly an invalid, as a paralytic and as frustrated dame-of-the castle" (242). Invalids also appear symbolically in a "neurotic octopus" who insists on devouring its tentacles and in Compostela's sculptured penguins, birds with clipped wings, like the spectators Adalberto observes—penguins laughing at penguins—at an art exhibit. Elda Astol's fantasized sublimation of her lover, the beleaguered sixteenth-century French heretic, cries out before his execution, "Freedom does not die! The cripples and invalids of spirit do" (235).

Symbolism is the only novelistic element which Laguerre consistently makes explicit and explains. Some symbols may be compared to the agressive tonic-key themes of music which alternate with more lyrical dominant-key themes that reappear as leitmotifs. The title of the novel has the general metaphorical value of interior passion, be it love, patriotism, creativity, and freedom in the positive sense, or mercantilism and false values in the negative sense. The suffocation of the affirmative fires of the spirit for lack of air to nurture the flames is made so clear that we will not enumerate all the appearances of the motif but simply assert that it is as recognizable as a major melodic motif in music. Not only is the book title symbolical, but also the majority of chapter headings, "Candles without Wicks," "Walls in the City" (prejudice), "Eve's Rib" (Ruth's influence on Pedro), "The Neurotic Octopus," "The Carrier Pigeon," "Coals of Passions," etc., some of them radiating like flames from the *Fire* of the main title.

Since events of the novel almost exclusively take place in urban settings, the only vestiges of nature seem to be those plants and animals appearing as metaphors. Juan Martínez Capó, in his review, cites this ample use of animal imagery which includes the oyster, fish, wasp, parrot, chicken, dove, cat, rat, dog, duck, monkey, and seahorse.[10] The children in the orphan asylum are referred to affectionately as "little animals"; New York is called a "jungle" and Harlem a "Zoo." Recurrent references to Cromagnon man and caves, initially used to characterize Pedro's life in New York, serve to remind us of the alternative civilized man faces in what may very well be a mirage of progress.

Just as a symphony may feature a certain type of instrument, the predominant instruments in *Fire and Its Air* are myths, stories about heroes, for as Adalberto affirms, "Peoples, no matter how materialistic they are, need to create myths," and Pedro agrees, "Yes, myth is the poetry of history and encourages the spirit" (250). Among the many universal, classical, and modern myths appearing in the novel, it is clear that native Puerto Rican myths have been "suffocated" in an "antiheroic country" (249) which demonizes History instead of deifying it, as Adalberto says. While other myths are amply described, those of Puerto Rico appear simply as brief allusions to Agüeybana, Guarionex, and Urayoán—Taíno chieftains who waged war against the Spanish conquerors; to Ponce de León, who searched for the Fountain of Youth and was first governor of the island; to the Puerto Rican captain Amézquita, who confronted the Dutch in 1625 and defeated them on the grounds of El Morro Fort; and to the valiant defenders of San Juan against British invaders in 1799, the Andino brothers and Pepe Díaz, the latter immortalized in a famous ballad.

The function of myths in the novel is determined by three major attitudes, the first of which is ironic demythification, which diminishes heroism by reducing it to a banal reality, a disillusion, contrasting with the original myth. Prometheus, who in Greek mythology stole fire from the gods to benefit man (hence a supporting element of the novel's title), is a sad, rusted hulk whose deck Pedro imagines as a map of Puerto Rico (whose outline indeed suggests a ship's deck). Native myths have been supplanted by American advertising myths and those of Hollywood ("boy-meets-girl," "poor-boy-gets-rich") and power (reducing Jupiter to Uncle Sam [37]); history is rewritten by the United States, counting the discovery of Puerto Rico from 1898, or by politicians counting it from their year of election. "The heroes of old are gone" (197), replaced by the great epic of Don Lorenzo Taveras, "Lord of the Cookies," with Lori as "Princess of the Cookie Empire" and a formidable "War of the Cookies." Ponce de León and Taíno chieftains yield their place to Javier Aguirre, "discoverer of Puerto Rico" (110), and to the "Great-Chief-of-the-Opulent Society" (164). Biblical demythification is also implied in Ruth, without the nobility of her namesake, but very much an Eve, and historical demythification in the baseness of Captain Sanrug's considering himself a Leif Ericson.

A second mode of using myths is through mythification which glorifies and ennobles reality and suggests illusion. Ulises is mythified by his name, that of the epic wanderer Ulysses or Odysseus, and by comparisons to Saint George against the dragon and to a "victim of a holy war as in medieval times" (129). The name of a minor character, Héctor Mejías, slain by Trujillo agents in New York because he could not bring himself to carry out the order to kill Ulises, brings to mind the fate of the hapless Trojan Hector. Pedro is diversely seen as a knight fighting dragons of prejudice, and a Prixos provoking the vengeance of the Argonauts in the invasion of Santo Domingo: "Perhaps he was seeking, in scale, the Deed that he dreamed for his country" (288). In Elda Astol's fancied former existence, Adalberto is the French Lutheran François Lanier, who defied the Catholic Establishment and died for his daring, and her love for Adalberto is given heroic stature, while the love story reflects her own past mistakes.

A third and last attitude toward myth may be called neutral in that it becomes a metaphorical comparison that neither diminishes nor glorifies, as when Ruth is called a Circe, Korea an Inferno, Puerto Rico's surrounding waters Limbo, and Pedro's self-devouring disillusion encouraged by Ruth "the dogs of Acteón" (set loose by the goddess Diana to devour their own master whom she had turned into a deer).

Myths serve to remind us of universality, for as Adalberto notes, *"Our life is born, like rivers, in the mountain. There is water from our rivers in all the seas and in the clouds that rain over all the lands of the world. I am universal for having been born in some point of this earth"* (126). Laguerre himself has acknowledged that the problems appearing in *Fire and Its Air* transcend the Puerto Rican context.[11] The quest for identity may be more generalized in this contemporary world than would be suspected by those who see it as their own national or continental problem, but *Fire and Its Air* is essentially a novel about Puerto Rican identity, individual and collective, past and future. Pedro José Expósito's discovery and acceptance of his identity which culminate in his generous impulse of self-realization, the regeneration of Don Lorenzo and María Luisa Taveras, and the deep love and social commitment of Adalberto Linares and Elda Astol are, in a generally pessimistic picture, upbeat notes on which the novel ends.

Chapter Eight
Full Circle and Beyond:
Benevolent Masters

Los amos benévolos [Benevolent Masters], published in 1976, contains many of the themes and techniques which give Laguerre's narrative its unique character, but at the same time there are new elements, both stylistic and thematic, that enrich the narrative and show that the author continues to develop in a constant spirit of experimentation and growth.

Part One, "A Candle to Light up the Day," begins with Damián Banderas's picking up a fare at the airport. He senses something strange about his female passenger, who is going to the home of his old friend and companion from the days of the workers' movement, Andrés Salanueva, who lives at 21 Teatro Street. There he converses with his old buddy, who informs him that the passenger he brought is his great-granddaughter Ludmilia, whom he believes killed in a plane crash soon after her interview on television with the magician Karim regarding her sighting of men from outer space. Before the flickering flame of a candle, recollections introduce themselves in the conversation either by thought or explicit speech of Lavidia, Andrés's wife, dead for twenty-three years, whose wonderful garden survives in the midst of urban development all about it and produces marvelous aromas out of season. We learn that Lavidia had considered herself a priestess of Micerino, who in ancient Egypt had incited the untouchable embalmers and the slaves who toiled on the Memphis pyramid to seek freedom.

Lavidia learned from Micerino the love of nature and true philanthropy. As Damián and Andrés sit before the television set, other pieces of the latter's family history are reconstructed. Andrés's adopted son Miguel Valencia, now a well-known lawyer and public figure, had rejected the spiritual sensitivity Lavidia tried to inculcate in him and had climbed to wealth and position through opportunism, betraying the workers he represented for personal gain and sacrificing his rich wife with his licentiousness. He drove his wife mad, alienated his effeminate son Osvaldito—who disappeared after an embarrassing episode with his aunt Leticia—and dedicated himself to pleasing the international set, particularly the American millionaire John Peterson. His business alliances with the latter and second marriage to Cecily Knight, sponsored by his "friend" eventually led to his economic ruin. The events on the "radiant screen" of the television, a gift to Andrés from Miguel Valencia's doctor son Germán, including a letter from a suffering wife and the magician's uncanny resemblance to Osvaldito, seem to mirror the details of the family history. Even the commercial sponsors, the perfumes *Comme il Faut* ("Proper," "conforming to social mores") and *Enfant Gâté* ("Spoiled Child"), suggest Miguel Valencia's social ambitions and egotism. He too is fascinated by Karim when his gluttonous housekeeper Maritoña turns on the program, for he perceives that the biography of his family is being aired on television.

The second part, "The Path of the Ants," presents events from the point of view of Miguel Valencia himself and at times from that of his son Germán, who resisted his attempts to make him into a society doctor and instead ministers to the slum poor. We learn that Miguel, the son of landowners routed by the Spanish Gonzaga family, was orphaned at two years of age and was taken in by his lazy Uncle Lisardo and his Aunt Carla (mother of Leticia), who represents for him the beginning of the "path of the ants" or threat of distruction which women in general pose. From the punishment which Carla inflicted upon him, he left for the strange spiritual world of 21 Teatro Street of Lavidia, and finally was able to rise to prominence. He is now, however, in the midst of a profound spiritual crisis and recognizes all the mistakes he committed to defend himself against women. He still prides himself for being a self-made man and for the legislation he had introduced against poverty and exploitation. Miguel has diabetes, which has put an end to his career as dilettante chef and gourmet, and he has renounced the pleasures he had sought before. Longing for peace and quiet, he stays home in the company of his housekeeper and her son Lenny Chang, both of whom he had brought from the Bronx, where the boy had been in trouble, involved in gang warfare. Miguel talks extensively with his son, offering him a "Last Supper" to take leave of his culinary hobby. He intends to salvage whatever is left of his fortune, severely reduced by alimony to Cecily Knight and by John "Junk's" schemes, to finance a hospital for indigent drug addicts, a pet project of Germán's. Miguel is deeply shaken by the Karim spectacle, convinced that Leticia, whom he considers basically responsible for Osvaldito's running away, has transformed the latter into the magician in order to maintain the devouring "path of the ants." He locks himself in his room for two days, but finally comes out to talk with Germán, who has just attended to a victim of gang violence, Alberto Gonzaga, of the same family which Miguel had vindictively violated and reduced to poverty. In the last scene Miguel Valencia observes the corpulent Maritoña watching the television screen, her back turned toward him and jaws moving as she eats, and feels himself compelled to kill her.

The brief third part of the novel, entitled "Requiem for a Dignitary," narrates subsequent events: the strangling of Maritoña, the arrival of Lenny—who stabs Miguel when he realizes he is the killer of his mother—and the police, followed by an encomiastic eulogy for the meritorious citizen Miguel Valencia, for inspiring in his son Germán a sense of social obligation, his dedication to culture, social legislation, economic development, and justice. As a "fitting tribute" to the great man's memory, three days of national mourning are declared. Of course Lenny Chang is execrated for the dastardly crime of killing his benefactor Valencia and nothing is said of the latter's involvement in Maritoña's murder, culminating the tremendous irony of this whole section.

Metaphorical Vision

Laguerre has a particularly perceptive way of discovering apt metaphorical expression in his novels. It is not the ornamental poetic metaphor or that of allegorical parallels but rather a way of envisioning what is happening in a metaphorical light and molding it into an unforgettable image. The extended metaphors found in Laguerre's fiction are a constant source of aesthetic pleasure. They seem to proceed so naturally and appropriately from the reality observed that there is never any hint of artificial contrivance, presenting a view that illuminates events very graphically, providing a sort of bridge between objective reality and the creative perception of it. Several of these metaphors are developed in *Benevolent Masters* as leitmotifs, notably the digestive system, beings from outer space, the path of the ants, Gullivers and dwarfs, and the title itself. Some of these are spelled out quite clearly for the reader while others require some analysis, in accordance with the tendency we have noted in Laguerre to offer something to readers on all levels.

In his classical book *Aspects of the Novel* the British author and critic E. M. Forster cites as a major fact of human life seldom given its due in novels that of food: "Food in fiction is mainly social. It draws characters together, but they seldom require it physiologically, seldom enjoy it, and never digest it unless specially asked to do so. Even poetry has made more of it—at least of its aesthetic side." Forster further observes that the individual

goes on day after day putting an assortment of objects into a hole in his face without becoming surprised or bored: food is a link between the known and the forgotten; closely connected with birth, which none of us remembers, and coming down to this morning's breakfast. Like sleep—which in many ways it resembles—food does not merely restore our strength, it has an aesthetic side, it can taste good or bad. What will happen to this double-faced commodity in books?[1]

Laguerre goes much further than even the possibilities formulated by Forster; he perceives the preparation, ingestion, digestion, and evacuation of food as a metaphor reflecting deepseated psychological anxieties of his protagonist. In the symbolical importance imparted to the digestive system, one of the least exploited areas of human life in literature, we are reminded of certain passages in Camilo José Cela's novel *La colmena* [The Beehive], in which the functions (or malfunctions) of digestion or elimination are symptomatic of the conditions of post–civil-war Spain.

First of all we learn that Miguel Valencia, by his own confession, enjoys preparing gourmet foods to lionize his American associates. The second section of the novel stresses the importance of this activity by which "Chef Michel" seeks to go beyond the insular limits of Puerto Rican cooking and becomes a universalist. He is proud of the fact that his stomach became a barometer of his yearnings for progress and for universalism. He recalls his special interest in learning about the lives of famous chefs and concedes that universal history can be told by that of gastronomical tastes, for spices were in great measure responsible for the discovery of America. His repudiation of native dishes parallels fondness for everything foreign, and therefore "universal," "I left Puerto Rican meals to the nationalist stomachs" (156).[2]

Miguel's fall from power and subsequent psychological crisis are reflected by digestive complications, sugar diabetes and a tapeworm. The first is highly ironic in view of the fact that sugar is a principal agrarian product of Puerto Rico and since Miguel as a lawyer had served the interests of the sugar barons, but even more than that, the disease suggests the inability of his spirit to appreciate his own country. This is subtly suggested by the diabetes, which is the failure of the body to provide something it needs, insulin, which enables it to utilize sugars and starches in order to generate energy.

Similarly, the tapeworm, which has been extirpated, returns phantasmally to haunt Miguel, who because of the common ailment feels linked to Louis XIV of France, whose court, it will be remembered, was the epitome of opulence and royal splendor in Europe. Miguel Valencia, too, had subscribed to an opulent life-style, but now he feels the tapeworm ensconced within him. It speaks to him, asserting, "My domain is your belly" (164). Miguel feels constant hunger but can only eat tasteless greens, and must avoid typical Puerto Rican food like the rice and beans he suddenly hungers for when separated from his island in New York. The tapeworm also assumes another dimension as it announces, "I became your Conscience, I have been your Conscience since long before I developed in your intestines and I will continue to be your Conscience as a phantom if you agree to let your son Germancito destroy me" (177).

Miguel Valencia's road to purification of spirit is accompanied by self-denial of starches and fats, symbolizing his renunciation of power and mundane pleasures, culminated by the "Last Supper" he prepares as anticipation of his "approaching retirement from the worldly life to live quietly and write verses" (193). He cooks a succulent Armenian dish for Maritoña, Lenny, and his son Germán while dining himself on "grass and vegetables." Stressing that he does not intend to parody the Last

Supper of Jesus, he notes the importance of inspiring spirit in what one eats or does not eat, and realizes how diet is related to country:

Look what happens in this tropical country: we eat as much fat as the Eskimos, it's difficult for us to maintain natural balance, we don't understand that the taste for one's country begins in the mouth. The pig may well be the symbol of that inconsistency. (196)

Germán, the physician, chides his father for not having done anything to correct that situation by initiating education so that by experiencing the "taste for country" in the mouth, it would lead to finding it also in the spirit. "You had the opportunity as a legislator," he asserts (197).

Another aspect of the digestive system arises in several episodes, that of elimination. Miguel's suffering wife puts a laxative in his drink before he is to go out with another woman; his associate the dwarf Tito Rodas laces all the drinks at a formal party with laxatives to embarrass the host, Miguel; and the latter prepares a gravy with urine to get even with an arrogant guest who belittled him. Yet another practical joke involving food occurs when Miguel serves his second wife coffee toasted with the blond hair he has shorn from her head to punish her for humiliating him.

Elimination is seen as the natural result of gluttony when Andrés Salanueva comments about Miguel Valencia that

his stomach was so long and wide it seemed to take over his whole body, and what a capacity for consuming food without getting fat! (Of course, this obliged him to return to the Earth a good part of what he had devoured, for some tribute had to be paid.) (110)

In the same dialogue Andrés recalls a founder of his own party who in order to take advantage of every moment planned acts of workers' liberation while evacuating on the "throne." Asked whether he considered the man less idealistically, Andrés answers that on the contrary, it only showed the human condition as an animal who must pay tribute to nature.

Another symbolical aspect of elimination may be found in the confession by which Miguel attempts to assuage his conscience. Germán fully understands the "cathartic attitude" of his father, his desire to expel the harmful elements that corrupt his serenity (248). Thus this part of the digestive process is seen in the novel in several lights, as a punishment, a relief, or simply as a reminder of man's animal condition.

The importance of the vast and varied metaphorical vision of food and digestion culminates in Miguel's last act when incited by the phantasmal Tapeworm and his insatiable hunger he kills his gluttonous housekeeper Maritoña. While she is basically an innocent victim her gusto in eating comes to represent that "mysticism of material satisfaction" which Miguel now repudiates.

Forster obviously was not thinking about the Hispanic tradition when he noted the infrequent use of food in novels, for Spanish authors have long used the picaresque novel, called "the novel of hunger," as a vehicle of social and moral denunciation. While Laguerre's novel cannot be classified as a picaresque novel in the traditional sense, it does retain the theme of hunger with symbolical overtones, uses the first-person narrative a good deal of the time, and may be said to portray a picaresque character in Miguel, an orphan who lives with several families and reaches "the pinnacle of all good fortune" (to quote Lazarillo de Tormes, the famous sixteenth-century pícaro) by his wits. Like Lazarillo, Miguel's "good fortune" is tremendously ironic, since the pícaro's marriage to a woman of dubious reputation and Miguel's similar situation are hardly enviable. Then too the very title of Laguerre's novel, *Benevolent Masters*, recalls that the pícaro is traditionally a servant of many masters, but it is significant to remember that the height of degradation for Lazarillo occurs when he serves the archpriest, the most benevolent of his masters (who, like John "Junk" Peterson in Laguerre's novel, arranges his marriage), because he consents to living a lie.

In conclusion it may be said that Miguel Valencia's hunger is existential (like nausea in Sartre), a metaphorical vision of his alienation from country, effective human relationships, and spiritual values.

Another metaphorical leitmotif is embodied in the beings from outer space whom Ludmilia purports to have seen in Sabana Grande in her interview with Karim on television. Reported sightings of the mysterious aliens have excited the collective curiousity and imagination. Damián Banderas relates this to a childhood fantasy of his son Quete about being leader of Operation Safari, whose object is to reach the great Spirodick Cavern (named in honor of the American geologist who supposedly discovered it but really a play on Spiro [Agnew] and Dick [for Richard Nixon]) where powerful monsters with human bodies and toads' heads called "expatriots" live. He had subsequently seen the word Safari written on a wall followed by the warning, "Toad-headed men, beware" (122). Andrés Salanueva perceives in his friend's story a subtle parable of those Puerto Ricans who follow Miguel Valencia's aspirations, rejecting all that is distinctly native: "I don't believe it's necessary to look very far to find them [the expatriots] because they're everywhere and the Spirodick cave may well cover 9,000 square kilometers. What's happening to Miguel is happening because of his stubborn toad's head . . ." (122).

The theme of aliens from space repeatedly suggests the alienation of Puerto Ricans like Miguel who do not feel at home on their own island and who live by values strange to their culture and tradition. Early in the novel Damián tells Andrés that "there is no worse fever than dilerium, not to know for what purpose you've been living on this Earth, or for what reason, to have created strange children, to create in yourself a stranger to your own kind" (20). In this sense Miguel is alien to his adoptive family as well as to the illegitimate granddaughter he has never seen, Ludmilia, but worst of all he experiences the anguish of being strange to himself, as Germán observes: "To travel around life without living in it is very painful. I try to make my acts live in my life and stop being satellites of myself" (213). He recognizes that he and his father live in two different worlds and that the latter has inhabited the kingdom of the Spirodicks. Thus the tremendous fascination the supposed visit from space creatures exerts on the public assumes an ironic dimension since their island is already inhabited by aliens, both foreign and native born.

The deferential attitude of Miguel Valencia and others of his type is designated throughout the novel by the metaphor of dwarfs and Gullivers, an allusion to Jonathan Swift's 1726 satire *Gulliver's Travels,* which attacks the vanity and hypocrisy of the court, statesmen, and political parties. Miguel's associate, the dwarf Tito Rodas, betrays and embarrasses him but in his own way wages war against the Gulliver giants while Miguel dedicates himself to serving them. By seeking the company of a dwarf, Rodas, he imagines himself another Louis XIV in command of his affairs but his unconditional submission to those who represent for him "universality" makes him a Lilliputian as far as Germán is concerned. Dwarfism, it is stressed, is more a state of mind than a strictly physical state. It comes from feeling small beside the foreign Gullivers.

Yet another metaphor appearing as a leitmotif is that of the title of the second section, "The Path of the Ants," in keeping with Laguerre's predilection for animal imagery. It is, however, a metaphor clearly spelled out for the reader by Miguel himself referring to those he thinks would destroy him. He feels that women have always perceived his weaknesses and taken advantage of them in a way comparable to that in which ants proceed toward a wounded grasshopper or toward a piece of sugar to be carried away. Ironically, Miguel rejects the female benefactors ("benevolent masters"?) of his orphaned childhood and adolescence—Aunt Carla, who never stopped reminding him of his debt, and even Aunt Lavidia, whose overwhelming kindness he found threatening—only to fall into the hands of other "benevolent masters" to whom he pays tribute as an adult.

Magical Realism

Emphasis on the fantastic, variously known as magical realism or the marvelous, so popular in the Latin American novel of the 1960s and 1970s and cultivated by Alejo Carpentier, Julio Cortázar, Carlos Fuentes, and Gabriel García Márquez, was late in coming to Puerto Rico. Dr. Edna Coll, in her speech of incorporation into the Puerto Rican Academy, made reference in 1979 to the novelists of more recent promotions, such as Pedro Juan Soto, Carmelo Rodríguez Torres, and Luis Rafael Sánchez, as those who use diverse forms of Surrealism, but does not mention Enrique Laguerre, undoubtedly because he had not previously been known for this modality and already was considered a "classical" author of the Generation of 1930.[3] With *Benevolent Masters,* however, Laguerre's name must be added to the list of cultivators of magical realism. The first part of the novel cannot help but remind the reader of García Márquez's magical and mythical world of Macondo in

Cien años de soledad [One Hundred Years of Solitude], but the Puerto Rican Macondo's magic is only perceptible to those who are attuned to it in the busy metropolis of San Juan. The aromas of roses and jasmines which mysteriously emanate from the garden of Lavidia creating spring in October are similar to those which come from the sea in García Márquez's "El mar del tiempo perdido" [The Sea of Lost Time]; The Egyptian sage Micerino's tutelage of the Salanuevas is somewhat like that of Melquiades in *One Hundred Years of Solitude;* and the presence of Lavidia, even though it is no longer physical, is as strong as that of the grand-matron Ursula in the same novel.

Laguerre's brand of magical realism, which indeed reminds us of that of García Márquez, is nevertheless unique in several respects. First of all, it coexists alongside the banal, materialistic, and obviously "realistic" world which Miguel Valencia prefers, although it does project itself into this world to some extent. This coexistence is clearly expressed by the division of the novel into its first two parts, each quite different. The first, whose setting is the house at 21 Teatro with Lavidia's garden, depicts this as a sort of magical island in the midst of a burgeoning metropolis with little appreciation for the type of experience the Salanuevas provide, although the rest of the people seem starved for fantasy, excited about the beings from outer space Ludmilia claims to have seen, but unable to see such things themselves. Perhaps their desire is simply to view the exotic, just as Miguel thinks that tourism may be served by importing foreign beauties, but Laguerre seems to remind us implicitly in his novel that one does not have to go to such extremes to appreciate the marvelous because it is part of the Puerto Rican heritage. The second part of the novel, while maintaining the mystery involving Karim and Osvaldito, provides a realistic portrayal of the incidents recounted in the first part.

The presentation of mystery is very subtle and not fully felt until well after Damián has arrived at Andrés Salanueva's house although he feels something strange from the beginning: "The afternoon was vibrant with presentiments but Damián Banderas accepted them without emotion, perhaps because he had lived too long, perhaps because solitude had been his companion for many years" (11). At 21 Teatro time does not exist and the voice of Lavidia speaks to Andrés, whose watch seems to symbolize this magical world, when its numbers leave their places and the hands have no place to turn to. The attitude of different characters toward the watch is revealing; for the practical Miguel "that watch is always stopped," while for Andrés "no one knows what time it is," which may have profound metaphysical implications.

The world of 21 Teatro is one of myths, as Zayas Micheli has pointed out.[4] There one may feel the presence of the Egyptian scribe and priest of ancient times, Micerino, the African Aiwel, and the Puerto Rican liberator of slaves Betances, who all represent timeless and universal currents of freedom, in the traditional way in which myths express human aspirations.

Laguerre's use of the fantastic leans more toward the mysterious than to the magical. The silver screen of the television Germán has for some strange reason given to Andrés as a gift projects several mysteries: the uncanny resemblance of the magician Karim to the long-disappeared Osvaldito and the multiple coincidences that make it seem that he is airing his family's history.

Despite the strong elements of magical realism which fill the first part of the novel with great poetic beauty, Laguerre's commitment seems to be essentially to realism and action. Andrés lives like a mummy alongside the ghosts of Lavidia, Micerino, and Betances, while Germán, influenced by them, manages to carry out real projects to implement his dream of a society in which everyone is equal and free.

A Spiritual Awakening

Significantly the title of the first section of *Benevolent Masters* is "A Candle to Light up the Day" and not, as would be expected, to light up the night, suggesting that the fundamental concern of the novel is to point out the need for illuminating the day, the daily life of people like Miguel Valencia who have given themselves over to the pursuit of material possessions and power and have turned their backs on other human values, like those revered at 21 Teatro, namely justice, freedom, and kindness.

The house is presided over by forces of the past, the voice of Lavidia, the spirit of Micerino, and the example of Ramón Emeterio Betances, whose portrait graces the foyer. Twenty-three years after her death Lavidia speaks to Andrés of respect for nature and of the timeless fountain of humanity represented by Micerino, who had befriended the untouchable embalmers of mummies preserved in order that the Ka or protective double could go into the afterlife. Micerino broke that taboo, endangering the Ka, but broke the dependence upon the material to achieve the spiritual.

Karim's purported genealogy points to the Spanish heritage, since he says he is the son of an Arab and a Spanish woman. He expresses his preference for Egypt and western Africa, making Damián recall his own family's origins in Africa, from which his ancestor Aiwel the hunter was carried by an antelope ghost to Memphis, where he was forced to work in the construction of the Great Pyramid. There Micerino implanted in the untouchables and slaves the breath of freedom, exposing himself to the ire of the Pharaoh and revealing the "Great Lie of the Ka passed by the powerful from generation to generation to exploit the poor" (52). Aiwel was inspired to escape far away and become a farmer to thank Ngewo: "They failed in their attempt to strip me of my primitive mystery and poison me with civilization" (52). This feat of liberation is again repeated on Puerto Rican soil with Betances's freeing the slaves, among them the father of Damián, Niño Banderas, whose surname symbolizes national pride in the flag. Betances also broke taboos, buying freedom rather than baptism for Niño Banderas. Lavidia tried to inculcate into her adopted son love for all helpless creatures and altruism, but to no avail.

Unusual in the Puerto Rican novel is the absence of partisanship, but in Laguerre the positive assertion of spiritual values takes precedence over any possible political ideologies. In this sense Germán, in the "realistic" second part, represents the same spiritual values sustained by Lavidia but carried out in an active campaign of charity toward the poor and underprivileged. Whereas Andrés Salanueva encloses himself as a mummy in his house of voices of the past, Germán as a doctor seeks to alleviate misery in the society about him with his own set of ethics, which enables him to live at peace with himself. He is, however, extremely tolerant of others' way of life, even that of his father. He seems to be, like Andrés, "one of those very rare common men who know how to be charitable naturally, who don't make a fuss about human weaknesses, because they know themselves to be very human" (68). Germán does not agree with his father, but neither does he reject him. Laguerre seems to regard very highly the value of dialogue and communication, as if to imply that the superior person has a certain moral obligation to sustain dialogue and hope that others will see the light. The message of "light and spirit" which Karim proclaims in a carnival atmosphere full of commercial exploitation is precisely what Puerto Rico on a course of material progress needs to recover from its roots in universal history (Micerino), Africa (Aiwel), and its own history (Betances). This can best be achieved in an atmosphere of true philanthropy, which, as Germán stresses, is free of all masters, even benevolent ones.

Germán's ideas about how changes should be brought about are nonviolent. He deplores the "ugly commerical tactics—scandal, posters, horrible 'murals'—they play into the hands of the Establishment, which tolerates them so there won't be any protests against their own similar methods" (214). Fully aware of the evils even in his own profession—the business of selling glands of the poor and using cadavers as vehicles of transporting drugs from Vietnam during that war—Germán continues to work toward his own ideals with hope and without bitterness. Others, like Ludmilia, look for spiritual values in cult religions, but Germán seems to provide a model for Laguerre's preferences.

Another spiritual value is the ability to appreciate nature. Although Laguerre's focal point is urban and not rural and despite the fact that descriptions of landscape are no longer usual in the narrative of the 1970s, the novel opens with a beautiful description of the sky as perceived by Damián Banderas, who raises his eyes above the urban landscape to appreciate the brilliant clouds illuminated by the setting sun. Villa Robles ("Oak Villa"), where Salanueva lives, is now filled with noises and carbon monoxide; vulgar neon lights block out the stars, and tall buildings the sunsets. In the struggle between nature and development, the latter appears to be winning except at 21 Teatro, where Lavidia's garden challenges the onslaught of time and "progress."

The story is told of Micerino's land, where the rains fell on Bilad-as-Sudan to swell the waters of the Nile as a sign of promise to the men who lived on the river's banks, and they were happy. The garden of Lavidia resists the contamination of the city and flourishes with the rains, conserving the life-giving current of Micerino's times. Andrés will not let Miguel and the developers replace his wooden home with a huge high-rise condominium. Nature in the novel is a scarce commodity, threatened by urban progress and appreciated only by those who possess a special sensitivity and are attuned to spiritual values uncorrupted by the material. It seems evident that Laguerre supports an affirmation of the values of human dignity, freedom, nature, and charity, and that he maintains an optimistic attitude that even those who have yielded to the System can change, though not always without traumatic effects.

Narrative Techniques

An introductory note announces that "each one of the first two parts of this novel is a novel in itself, although both have a common denouement: the third part." While this flexibility of choice reminds us of a similar procedure in Julio Cortázar's *Rayuela* [Hopscotch], it is obvious that most readers will begin with the part which comes first in the book. The effects of interchanging the parts becomes a predominantly intellectual matter to be examined in a second reading, for certain considerations come into play when the parts are shuffled. Reading in the order of presentation provides an initially unfavorable picture of Miguel Valencia, predisposing the reader to view him as an opportunist and cad. With the second part, in which the point of view is that of the protagonist himself for the most part, the reader is inclined to sympathize with him as he undertakes the difficult path to contrition. The explanation behind the despicable behavior commented upon in the first part also helps to diminish the reader's disdain for him. The short and surprising third part has greater impact at this point because we have seen Miguel's improvement just before the crime. If the order of reading is reversed the murder of Maritoña is less surprising since we have just been immersed in all his other "crimes," but then the praises heaped upon him in public after his death become even more ironical in contrast. In any case, we see alternate modes of reading more as a narrative technique to "open" the novel and give it flexibility than as an integral, necessary part of the novel.

The combination of the three parts allows a multi-perspective view of the protagonist, first presented by two humble characters sympathetic to him on a human level but appalled by his lack of values, then by Miguel Valencia himself with the added perspective of his son Germán, and finally by "the public," which ironically designates him as a model citizen, supported by the hypocritical comments of his "friends."

The narrative employs the most sophisticated novelistic techniques with ease and naturality. The novel's epigraph is supplied by the fictional character Germán, who autonomously steps out of the book to provide a statement about his father's association with Louis XIV, tapeworms, and comic dwarfs. Dialogue is incorporated into the narration without the trappings of explicit speaker identification. Some dialogues, like those of Lavidia, whose phantasmal presence is felt by Andrés, are in italics, but others, whether they be interior monologues or involve changes in speakers, are simply encrusted in the text so naturally that there is no confusion or difficulty in following the reading or in identifying the speaker. Laguerre continues to write for a wide range of readers, utilizing modern novelistic techniques in a way that can be accessible to an audience which is not exclusively intellectual. The narrative flows at a fast pace with a high degree of mystery and suspense so that the reader's interest never falters.

Miguel Valencia's psychology is carefully and convincingly developed although some stereotyping occurs in characterizing Cecily Knight (blond American opportunist) and John "Junk" Peterson (unscrupulous American millionaire), ironically comparable to the stereotyping of the Latin image in the United States. The balance among the diverse elements which compose the novel makes it possible to categorize it, if one should wish to do so, as either a social, psychological, or mystery novel, but it is in fact all these and more.

Full Circle

One of the most surprising aspects of *Benevolent Masters*, forty-one years removed in time and experience from Laguerre's first novel, *The Blaze,* is that it seems to respond to similar concerns, revealing great continuity in our author's creation despite changed circumstances and settings. In retrospect it is quite startling to read Antonio Pedreira's comment, *"The Blaze* is the novel of one of our most grave illnesses: collective diabetes," anticipating in fact the image developed in *Benevolent Masters.*[5] Miguel Valencia cannot utilize "the bad weed" any more than the peons of *The Blaze,* whose energy is likewise sapped by the uncontrollable cane.

In both novels, too, there are masters—cruel, heartless, and demanding masters in *The Blaze* who reduce the jíbaro to slavery, and now benevolent masters, served willingly in the later novel. Like Don Flor and Juan Antonio Borrás, Miguel Valencia is proud of being a "self-made man"; like Juan Antonio he finds himself hungry for distances, hemmed in by buildings and power instead of mountains and the sea.

In Laguerre's first novel we find the sensation of alienation when Juan Antonio realizes that "often we wander far away from ourselves" and states, "How often I have dreamed of renouncing this miserable life of tourists in our own land!"[6] In both novels nature is capable of reviving the spirit and sunsets are the favored moments. In *The Blaze* the mountains provide a refuge from the barbaric civilization Juan Antonio shuns; in *Benevolent Masters* Lavidia's garden is all that is left of nature in the urban environment. And in the two novels, despite their great differences, the protagonists are essentially jíbaros who have allowed themselves to be corrupted by "barbaric" models, alienating themselves from family, traditions, values, and self. True to his own literary roots, Laguerre's fiction may be said to have come "full circle" while at the same time progressing notably in its scope, technique, and concerns. Circumstances have changed greatly in Puerto Rico since 1935. Laguerre no longer postulates just a return to jíbaro tradition of yesteryear but, while decrying Miguel's misguided notions of "universality," recognizes true universal currents which, joined by native influences, may fortify the Puerto Rican to make him, like Germán, his own man.

Chapter Nine
Theater, Short Stories, and Essays
The Resentful Woman

La resentida [The Resentful Woman], Laguerre's only published play, represents his contribution to the Generation of 1930s' attempt to stimulate native culture, in response to Emilio S. Belaval's call for a truly Puerto Rican theater.[1] After the shortlived but valiant efforts of the Areyto group ended in 1941, the University Theater became an important project, although Spanish and international dramatists were its usual fare. In 1944, however, *The Resentful Woman* was presented on April 12, 13, and 14 to a total audience of 10,000 people. The theater subsequently closed its doors to Puerto Rican playwrights until 1956, when, thanks to the efforts of Nilda González, two works of Francisco Arriví were performed. Soon after, in 1958, the Institute of Puerto Rican Culture began the annual Festival of Puerto Rican Theater, with Laguerre's play performed in the second festival, in 1959. Arriví refers to the first trial run of the play in 1944 as a brave experiment which "confirmed, as later in the festivals sponsored by the Institute of Puerto Rican Culture, that an ample Puerto Rican conscience exists in search of its artistic definition."[2]

The first act of *The Resentful Woman* finds Doña Marta impatiently silencing the lamentations of Ma Valenta, her old nursemaid and servant, while her stepdaughter Rosario nervously awaits the arrival of her Spanish sweetheart Alfredo, fearful of the seditious bands which have been preying upon Spaniards. Marta complains that neither her husband Esteban nor Rosario loves her and says she is not to blame for not having children. They hear a ballad sung by a farmhand about Marta's brother Sotero Cintrón's capture by the rural police. Marta's nephew Cecilio, son of Sotero, is in love with Rosario, who considers him a brother, and he threatens her if she allows Alfredo to continue his visits. Esteban arrives and sends Cecilio to meet Alfredo on the way, to Rosario's dismay and Marta's protests.

In the second act Marta and her husband have a rather hostile discussion filled with ambiguities, recriminations, and allusions to her resentment toward the rural police and the *Compontes* of former years. Rosario has a nightmare in which she sees Cecilio staring at her and hears a cry in the night. Cecilio returns alone to report that Alfredo stayed home, but Esteban notices blood on the cape he had been wearing. Alfredo's father Don Rodrigo, at one time a rural policeman, seeks refuge at Esteban's farm because his was burned by the marauders, but he assumes Alfredo is sleeping. The faithful worker Eustaquio tells Esteban he found Alfredo's riderless horse and that Cecilio has fled; a peon brings Cecilio's knife, found near the dying Alfredo, who refused to reveal the name of his killer.

The final act begins eight days later. Esteban has organized a group of men to combat the abuses of the seditious bands. He and Marta again exchange hostilities as she alludes to fifteen years of bitterness, silence, and resentment. A message is thrown through a window that Cecilio will come to get what is his. In the second scene of the act, Ma Valenta inadvertently reveals that Cecilio is really Marta's son, which prompts the latter's full confession that a rural policeman had assaulted her and that she had been subsequently abandoned by her family, except for her brother Sotero and her mother. She almost died in childbirth and the doctor considered it unlikely that she could have more children. She realizes that her hatred toward the Spanish police influenced Cecilio and has resulted in his being pursued as a killer. Esteban promises not to harm her son and Marta, relieved by her confession, now treats old Ma Valenta with tenderness. In Esteban's absence Cecilio comes to carry away Rosario. Marta tries to dissuade him and he explains how he came to kill Alfredo, although he had intended only to join the *tiznaos* to avenge the death of his father at the hands of the Spanish rural police. Marta's confession that he is her son falls on deaf ears, and on hearing the voice of one of Esteban's men, Cecilio slaps Marta who defends Rosario. In a desperate effort to prevent her son from abducting the girl, she grabs his revolver and shoots him.

The Resentful Woman, together with the novel *The Fingers of the Hand* (1951), are the only books by Laguerre which feature a female protagonist. Before writing this play, he had directed his attention mainly toward the man's world in *The Blaze, Montoya Plantation,* and *The 30th of February,* although his portrayal of women had been sympathetic in those novels. Doña Marta justifies the new focus eloquently when she states, "You men only think of yourselves. We women don't count, we are nothing, we do not suffer in the flesh" (106).[3] Laguerre's dramatic interest in portraying the female psyche recalls Ibsen's *Hedda Gabler,* but even more so Benavente's strong female characters in the rural drama *Señora Ama* [The Respected Lady of the House] and in *La malquerida* [The Unloved Girl], whose title in Spanish seems to echo in that of *La resentida.*

The play is set against the historical background of the days following the United States takeover of Puerto Rico when seditious bands roved the countryside burning the farms of Spaniards and their sympathizers, at the same time satisfying personal grievances in an arbitrary fashion against fellow Puerto Ricans. This is seen when a jíbaro asks Don Esteban to loan his boss a shotgun to protect himself against the *tiznaos* and *comevacas* (thus called because they blackened their faces and ran off cattle), and Esteban, incensed that a Puerto Rican should be the object of persecution, forms a group of men to try to impose order. The ballad about Ramú, the heartless rural policeman who tied up the valiant Sotero Cintrón, Marta's brother, which the jíbaro Eufemio learned at a wake, alludes to the abuses committed around the time of "the terrible year of '87," treated at length in *The Undertow.* The seditious bands appear in the same novel and also in *Montoya Plantation.*

The plot is simple and forceful, as is the theme, that violence breeds violence. It is the legacy of "the terrible year of '87" erupting twenty-two years later. Marta's final act puts an end to the chain which would have made Rosario another Marta. Her story is as old as Europa, who in Greek mythology was carried off by Jupiter and subsequently gave birth to a monster, the Minotaur. It will be recalled that an assault serves as justification for the behavior of Doña Bárbara in Rómulo Gallegos's famous novel. The old Spanish code of honor pinned men's honor largely on the purity of the family women, a rather unique and unfortunate custom which gave rise to many a plot in the history of the Spanish theater. We can appreciate the unfairness of such norms when, as in Marta's case, the woman is not at fault. Certainly her being repudiated by her father and brothers, other than Sotero, added insult to injury. She even feels repudiated by the Virgin, to whom she has prayed fervently to be able to bear a child for Esteban. The psychological and even physical mutilation resulting from her experience has cast its shadow many years later, even projecting itself into the next generation. Modern sociology has recognized only recently the distrust to which the female victim is subjected and the shame that makes the ordeal difficult to discuss; crisis centers have been set up in which victims may speak to other women. Laguerre's play is surprisingly perceptive in anticipating these ideas, for we can see how quickly Rosario sympathizes with Marta while Esteban, visibly moved by the confession, cannot bring himself to grant her "forgiveness." Marta's final act responds to her determination not to let the same thing happen to Rosario and, in sacrificing her own son to save the girl, she proves her love for her stepdaughter.

There is a great deal of dramatic irony in the fact that innocent people suffer for wrongs they did not commit. Early in the play Esteban asks whether his friend Rodrigo is to blame for what the bad Spaniards did (14); in the second act Don Rodrigo asks Esteban if it is right for him to have to pay for the crimes his government committed (63); and in the last act Esteban recognizes the injustice of the innocent having to pay for the sinners (93). Yet Laguerre seems to say that no one can consider himself innocent who has not tried to overcome resentment for wrongs inflicted upon him. Perhaps Cecilio's propensity toward violence and Marta's embitterment might have been tempered by affection. As Marta tells Rosario, "Cecilio needed affection. . . . I tell you the lack of affection is the worst of hungers" (98). It is not clear to what extent Esteban is guilty of this with regard to Cecilio. He shows consideration on two occasions, when he tells him to take his cape because it looks like rain and when he asks him whether he has eaten upon the young man's arrival after searching for Alfredo. Eustaquio assures Esteban that the latter has been like a father to Cecilio, but this is not obvious in the play. In portraying herself as a victim Marta disclaims any responsibility for her problems but recants in the closing words of the play: "I brought up a beast and I am to blame. I myself am to blame. God help me! . . . My son!" Her greatness lies in this acknowledgment, while the other characters cannot perceive that they too are equally innocent and guilty.

Marta is in many respects comparable to the classical tragic hero driven by the "tragic flaw" of her resentment and by a fateful aftermath of her original suffering to a situation which elicits the classical sentiments of terror and compassion. Also reminiscent of Greek tragedy is the strong unity of the play, the three acts of which take place in the living room of Esteban's house; the play follows the theme with no digressions and covers a period of only eight days. Ma Valenta assumes the functions of the Greek chorus as a harbinger of misfortune in all three acts, alluding to secrets she has kept hidden, expressing her worries because "evil is loose," and fearing to stay alone because "the rural police are after Cecilio." These lamentations, as well as the clouded sky of the first two acts, Rosario's nightmare and premonitions in the second, and the ballad about Sotero all forbode impending tragedy. The use of the ballad here recalls similar foreshadowing in Lope de Vega's well-known play *El caballero de Olmedo* [The Nobleman of Olmedo] as the hero makes his way home on a trip that is his last. Starting with the absence of Alfredo's name from the cast of characters, the reader has little doubt as to the young man's fate. For a while we even suspect Esteban of being overconfident in his peon Eustaquio, but there are no surprises. As in Greek tragedy, we are prepared to expect the worst and it inexorably occurs, with the confirmation of fears and suspicions nurtured from the very beginning. Even Marta's confession comes as no shock to the alert spectator or reader, since the secret is insinuated in Ma Valenta's laments, in Esteban's reticences, in the ambiguities of his conversations with Marta about the first days of their marriage, and in a quick slip of the tongue at the close of the first act when Marta berates her husband for sending her nephew out on such a bad night: "My son is not going to receive the blows another deserves" (39).

The play is an excellent piece of dramatic craftsmanship in which the novelist yields to the playwright, for there are no digressions, long speeches, or descriptions as we might expect in the work of an author who is primarily a novelist. In contrast to the changing settings we find in Laguerre's novels, he confines himself here to only one interior, with surrounding nature suggested in the golden sun seen over the peaks of the mountain and references to the coffee plantation of Esteban. The jíbaro character is totally suggested in the dialogue of rarely more than two or three sentences, in conformity with the customary reticence and fatalistic attitude of the jíbaro, a man of few words. There is faithful rendering of country speech, with some degree of "jibarisms" appearing in the uneducated Cecilio and to a greater degree in the peons and in Ma Valenta. Metaphorical allusions to native flora and fauna are common:

Esteban: . . . You are always hiding old yaguas [a native palm]. (49)
Marta: Another girl eats the orange and you have insisted that his [Cecilio's] teeth be set on edge. (39)
Esteban: . . . I'll watch out for him as for a dog who gets into a corn patch. (89)
Rosario: These days the sun seems more yellow than ever and burns in my eyes as the juice of the orange. (95)

The longest dialogues are those of Marta in the last act, meeting with the wounding brevity of Esteban's terse answers.

Dramatic irony is evident in the lack of communication between husband and wife, alienated by misunderstanding; in Esteban's expectations that Marta be a mother to his daughter while he has not fulfilled her expectations toward Cecilio; in Esteban's scorn for her as a barren woman when it is precisely because she was not barren that Cecilio was born; and in the latter's hatred toward the Spaniards, not knowing that his father was one. Additional irony appears in the accompaniment of nature, in consonance with events, which in the first two acts turns threatening, then stormy, and finally clear, with a sun that irritates the eyes just as the truth does the heart when Marta tells her story at the end.

Laguerre refrains from symbolism in the play, though it is a characteristic of his novels, perhaps because he considers it difficult for the general spectator to grasp in the theater.[4] Two lyrical metaphors are expressed by Rosario in referring to "Sunday's arrival" as that of her beloved and in her wish to be able to replace hopes and dreams as easily as she replaces fresh flowers for the withered ones at her mother's portrait.

One further question to be dealt with is Francisco Arriví's observation of "touches of melodrama," a judgment repeated by other critics.[5] Within the context of the total work we feel this is not the case; actually emotion is contained and dominated until the very end. Before the reality of Alfredo's death Esteban is indignant but stoical, and Rosario controls her grief with dignity. We detect no exaggerated accumulation of sentimentality calculated to move the audience to tears, no maudlin display or mawkishness. In the last act Marta's confession generates emotion, in perfect accord with the traditional tendency of women to manifest emotion outwardly, but she instantly repels Esteban's pity and dominating herself inquires almost casually whether he is hungry. Finally, the violence of the closing scene is justified by the character of Cecilio (aided, perhaps, by heredity and upbringing) and the resolute nature of Marta. The pathos resulting from the situation seems justifiable, and in the terror and compassion elicited by these humble rural Puerto Ricans there is much of the legitimate catharsis that Greek tragedy sought to achieve.

Short Stories

Laguerre considers most of his short stories preliminary sketches for novels rather than works written precisely for that genre. Seven stories were written prior to the publication of *The Blaze,* four soon after, one in the 1940s and three in the 1950s. Only four of his short stories have been republished in anthologies following their initial publication in periodicals: "Raíces" [Roots], "Pacholí," "El enemigo" [The Enemy], and "Naufragio" [Shipwreck]. "Roots" appears in several anthologies, probably because it conveys the spirit of his novels in brief. In accordance with Laguerre's own preference, we shall treat only the four works which he considers true short stories independent of possible plans for novels.

"Roots" (1937) is about José Rafael, a country boy unsuited for the law profession he chooses who returns to the family home for the burial of the old family peon, the jíbaro Pedro, whose last wish was for José Rafael to be true to his people. Attracted by the glorious beauties of nature and the friendship of his childhood companion, José Rafael decides to stay. As at the end of *The Blaze,* the young man returns to his roots. The end of the story is exemplary and is obviously a reflection of the author's own intimate concern: "He felt himself a hungry tree sucking up the land. He imagined that the hands of Pedro were roots that from the hot soil held him and nourished him" (192).[6] The plot is one which is basic to Laguerre's novels, the search for oneself and authenticity, usually related to a return to nature. In the shorter genre there is more opportunity for the reader to note the lyrical and original descriptions of nature: "In the midst of some clouds there was a puddle of sky—holy water in which God wet the finger to bless the day" (192). As in *The Blaze,* nature and people intermix, with Pedro becoming roots and the father's embrace that "of the land, close, with live palpitating of heart and flowering of hopes" (191).

The return to nature is also a return to the innocent delights of childhood which makes the young man think of life rather than death. He is still young enough to recover his past without trauma, in contrast to the protagonists of Laguerre's later novels. The jíbaro Pedro is described in such a way that the reader cannot help but think that he really existed for the author. "Roots" is evidently a story which is dear to Laguerre, since he includes it in two anthologies he himself edited, as well as in others. The collective first-person plural communicates a sense of national pride; describing Pedro's burial, Laguerre speaks of wooden boards "made from the heart of our trees" and of Pedro as "a legitimate son of our mountains" (187–88). The story belongs roughly to the period of *The Blaze,* but contains elements which appear in other novels, such as the mentorship of an older man (*Montoya Plantation*), allusions to frivolous university life later developed in *The 30th of February,* and the renunciation of a career in the city, later seen in *River Bed without a River* and *Benevolent Masters.* It is certainly the most representative of his short stories.

"Pacholí" (1950) is for me Laguerre's finest story, perfectly adjusted to the genre in its concentration, view of one moment in three lives, and poignant irony. The narrator is a schoolmaster who feels an inexplicable sadness and dissatisfaction with what he feels he should be and is not. In the next section of the story a broken man, more dead than alive, approaches him and asks his help in requesting admittance to a hospital where he can die. To the narrator's surprise, their conversation reveals that this poor soul is his old childhood companion Pacholí, broken by work in the sugar fields, misfortune, and tuberculosis. In answer to Pacholí's observation that he must be a happy man, the narrator responds negatively. Like so many protagonists in Laguerre's novels, the narrator lives a life not in accord with his real inclination to be closer to nature, but the alternatives seem equally disappointing, to judge by Pacholí and the sad, barefoot woman who passes by, the object of their youthful dreams not that many years before.

The story presents contrasts between the way of speaking of the schoolmaster and the jíbaro and their lives, yet the two are ironically alike, one broken physically, the other spiritually. The narrator presents Pacholí's dialogue both directly and indirectly, sprinkled with jíbaro expressions. Introspection alternates with dialogue, the past with the present. The story's universal dimension portrays sadness before the passing of time, the childhood paradise when, "before, we three were the happiest creatures on earth. Today we didn't recognize each other."[7] There is also social comment implicit in the description of the conditions which caused Pacholí's premature decline. The bipartite structure is similar to that of *Montoya Plantation* and *River Bed without a River*, with the first part establishing here a tone of vague sadness as a prelude to the meeting of the narrator with Pacholí. The story is open ended in its conclusion and perfectly suited for the shorter genre, with lyrical, contemplative, and ironic impact.

"The Enemy" (1956), considered Laguerre's best story by Concha Meléndez, relies on psychological verisimilitude, situation, and a shocking ending.[8] Narrated in the third person, the narrator nevertheless assumes the point of view of the protagonist Isabel, who on returning from her honeymoon tries to stay awake until her husband, who must work nights for two weeks, comes home. In her half-awake condition, she almost forgets that she is now away from her hated stepfather. She had grown up in fear of his drunkenness, ill treatment of her mother, and sadism in destroying letters from Isabel's beloved Juan Manuel, her only ideal and hope for rescue from a horrible home situation. For years she had slept in fear of her stepfather's entering her room, and she kept her father's old revolver under her pillow. Her suffering finally ended with the return of Juan Manuel, their elopement, and new home. Unable to stay awake, Isabel falls asleep but she hears the door and sees the homicidal arms of her stepfather extended toward her. Shots ring out, there is a cry, and she awakes to find she has shot her husband. The mosquito netting over the nuptial bed showed "two burned spots like enemy eyes that look through mist" (143).

The end of the brief story has tremendous impact; it is paradise lost as soon as it was found. The theme of the damage adult cruelty and insensitivity can do to children is also present in *The Fingers of the Hand*

(1951) and in several of Laguerre's essays. The figure of the feared stepfather in the story recalls the scar left on Lucrecia Madrigal's emotional makeup by the violence of her Uncle Pedro and her feelings of being abandoned by her real father's death. The setting in the short story, however, is not geographically important. The end is a result of the lasting effects of years of an unhealthy home atmosphere combined with coincidence, all within the realm of possibility.

"Shipwreck" (1959) is also a departure from Laguerre's novelistic techniques in that character development is not particularly important and ironic impact is stressed.[9] Gabriel, a young wanderer, eighteen years of age, finds himself on a small island where he is befriended by the old "patriarch" Pedro, but nonetheless feels the collective hostility of the approximately fifty men, women, and children who inhabit the isolated place, with the exception of an attractive girl, Rosina, sister of Juan Domingo. Gabriel cannot understand why the latter and the other islanders react so strongly when he sits on a rock above the "Devil's Pool" until Pedro tells him about the Man of the Island, who had hidden a treasure gotten by a pact with the devil in the cave below, where he had drowned when it was invaded by the sea. He explains that outsiders bring misfortune and recounts the legend of the Dead Man's Shrub, a dwarfed tree above the cave. An outsider who had heard the story about the treasure made friends with Jesuso, the father of Juan Domingo and Rosina. He secretly tied a rope around the base of the small tree to lower himself down the precipice to the cave and when Jesuso tried to stop him, supposedly pushed him into the pool, where he drowned. The people of the island no longer covet the devil's treasure; the stranger had disappeared.

Gabriel, recalling his "hunger of generations," his infancy and childhood abandoned by his father, Baldomero Rojas, an adventurer, and his harsh aunt's calling him as lazy as his father, proposes to Rosina and suggests their leaving the island after he takes the treasure. At low tide, he ties a cord around the shrub which during the dangerous descent gives way. Falling into the pool, he grasps the chain of a rusted anchor left from some shipwreck, the only thing to be found in the cave, as Rosina calls for help. The old patriarch Pedro, disillusioned with the young man, comments that it was as if he were paying for the death of Jesuso years before at the hands of the greedy stranger, who, as it turns out, was Baldomero Rojas, the boy's father. Two nights later Gabriel leaves the island, alone.

The story is fast-paced and sets us up for the surprising and ironic revelation at the end that Gabriel is indeed the son of the man who brought misfortune to Rosina's father. The atmosphere of superstition, legend, and mystery complements the carefully structured plot. There is lyricism in the description of the attraction exercised by the green waters and the green eyes of Rosina. The coastal setting is similar to that of the second part of *The Ceiba Tree in the Flower Pot,* published three years later, but as we have indicated, geography is less important than the fact that greed and the challenge of hidden treasures are all too universal, making plausible the ironic repetition of a frustrated attempt to steal the devil's treasure.

Essays

Laguerre's extensive essay production consists of journalistic and professional articles, prologues, lectures, and radio transmissions on a wide variety of subjects. He began writing for magazines and journals in 1932 and has used such pseudonyms as Gustavo Montiel, Tristán Ronda, Alberto Yunque, and Luis Uroyán.[10] The latter was assumed at the same time as the publication of *The Undertow,* in which the Taíno chieftain Urayoán figures so prominently. We shall treat only the essays published in books with emphasis on those which reveal discursively his values and ideas and which elucidate his fictions.

La poesía modernista en Puerto Rico [Modernist Poetry in Puerto Rico], presented as a thesis for the master's degree at the University of Puerto Rico in 1941 and published in 1969, continues to be an oft-cited source in the field. Here Laguerre shows his abilities both as a scholar and writer, handling an immense quantity of investigative material and synthesizing it into a thoroughly readable presentation which can be enjoyed by the specialist and nonspecialist alike. Unusual in this type of thesis is the extraordinary critical acumen of the author in appraising artistic and human values in the poetry studied.

The book begins with the origins of Modernism and the precursors and models which influenced the flowering of the movement in Puerto

Rico from 1913 to 1916. Laguerre notes the influence of Darío and Santos Chocano in the great "novels of the land" of Spanish America, revealing that his interest in Puerto Rican Modernism is not an arbitrarily chosen thesis topic but rather a matter of personal urgency and relevance for the young novelist. It becomes more and more apparent that an important by-product of the scholarly study is the investigation of the author's own immediate cultural past. It isn't until much later in the book that he states unequivocally that the roots of that past "penetrated the stratum of our conscience as a people" (188), that same conscience which vibrates in all his novels. The critic establishes his preferences with regard to some aspects of Modernism: "We admire the abandonment of clichés, its rhythmic renovations, lexical enrichment, attractive novelty, realization of musicality, genuine expression, assurance of a personality" (19), he says, but expresses his dislike of excessive eroticism, false religiosity, sybaritism, superficial aristocracy, intellectual neurosis, frivolous epicurism, and exoticism.[11]

The study considers José de Diego's renovation of poetry in the Modernist vein after 1890, the consequences of the change of government in Puerto Rico fomenting nostalgia for Spain but also interest in native themes, and the influence of *La Revista de las Antillas* [The Magazine of the Antilles]. He studies individual authors, pointing out themes, style, distinguishing characteristics, and biographical data, for "there is no doubt that the lives of poets are reflected in their works. . . . Personal experience is inevitable in all artistic creation" (91). Included in that experience are observations, readings, and reflections. Laguerre's in-depth analyses suggest that profundity, originality, and sincerity are qualities he admires in literature.

It is interesting to note Laguerre's attitude toward politics in criticism and in literature. He confesses himself reluctant to "speak of politics in a study of poetry" but finds it inevitable to do so here (61). In his chapter about Luis Lloréns Torres, the "Walt Whitman of Puerto Rico," he treats political aspects only briefly, since he finds the poet stronger than the politician in his verses. It cannot escape the reader of Laguerre's novels that some of his inspiration must certainly have come from this poet whom the critic admires for his use of historical, biblical, and mythological allusions, musicality, folklore, regionalism, popular motivation, and Hispanic and native historical consciousness, although he attributes many of these procedures to the poet's political sentiments.

It would serve no purpose in this brief study of Laguerre's book to summarize the information it provides, but the relevance of his investigation to his own activity as a novelist can hardly be underestimated. His study of the apogee of Modernism is followed by that of its rapid decline after 1916, a description of the vanguard movements of the 1920s, and the advent of the magazine *Indice,* which posed the questions of Puerto Rican identity and problems for the next generation, which is his own. Modernism generated artistic consciousness, a healthy eclectic course, and universal interest nurtured in Puerto Rico by native concerns. For Laguerre "the greatest fecundity of our Modernism does not lie in having followed. . . . [superficial] tendencies, but in the desire for renovation; in an awakening of the Puerto Rican conscience; in the enthusiasm for culture; in the explorations of our nature; in love for the language, traditions and roots of our origin; in a healthy universalism (179)." These innovations outlived Modernism and left their imprint upon Laguerre and his generation.

Pulso de Puerto Rico [Pulse of Puerto Rico], published in 1956, is a selection of essays originally broadcast on radio station WIPR during the period from 1952 to 1954, which Laguerre considers one of great political and cultural transition.[12] The book contains eight thematic sections about the press, Puerto Rican history, tourism, education, language and literature, folkloric expression, art institutions, and research. To summarize the content of the almost fifty essays which comprise the volume would be virtually impossible and in any case would not do justice to the careful development of ideas. The book does, however, represent an implicit statement of philosophy on diverse subjects and sheds light on many motivations in his fiction, although it should not restrict reader interpretation of his works.

A major theme of *Pulse of Puerto Rico* is the need for the study of the island's history in order to correct the collective evil of evasion, which manifests itself in blind admiration for everything foreign. Laguerre praises the efforts of historians and intellectuals like Ricardo Alegría, Arturo Morales Carrión, and Manuel García Cabrera in fomenting consciousness of Puerto Rican culture but points out what remains to be done. He suggests infusing literature with native history and myths (which, of course, is what he does in his fiction). He stresses the importance of restoring Old San Juan and preparing descriptive materials with history "seasoned" by legend to attract and enlighten tourists while at the same time developing native culture ("History and Legend," "Old San Juan," "Tourism"). Laguerre sees Governor Muñoz Marín's trip to the United States in 1949 as inaugurating a new era of offering cultural favors instead of requesting economic ones ("Seminar of History"). In various essays he discusses folkloric expression as a source of cultural pride and he urges public and official support for efforts to foment dance, crafts, music, and cultural projects. Accepting extensive emigration to the mainland as a reality, he views historic consciousness as important in preparing the emigrants as vocational and technical training.

Another question which Laguerre treats is that of the universality of island concerns: "Do our problems have to be small because we are geographically small? Don't we worry about the world's problems when we worry about those of our land? Are we separated from the world?" ("The University," 170). He concludes that "when we worry about our problems, indeed we worry about the serious problems of the world, being ourselves part of the world" (173), words quite similar to those of Adalberto Linares in *Fire and Its Air*.[13]

Laguerre's novels constantly show that few people are all bad or all good, something he clarifies in discussing "Textbooks and Supplementary Reading": "There is an educational matter which has always bothered me: the influence that children's stories have upon the lives of future adults" (195). He finds that stories like "Cinderella" provoke dissatisfaction, evasion, and a false concept of life and recommends greater relevance and mixture of good and evil. He states that *The Fingers of the Hand* was inspired by the desire to show the bad effects of adult pressures upon children which communicate to them their frustrations, hatreds, limitations, ancestor cult, and hysterias, not only in Puerto Rico but in other countries as well ("Some Ideas about Criticism").

Of particular interest are Laguerre's ideas about literature and criticism. In treating works by Arriví, Marigloria Palma, René Marqués, Samuel Lugo, Julia de Burgos, and Ester Feliciano Mendoza, he proceeds inductively, noting characteristics and sometimes defects, without any dogmatic preconceptions. He attacks the mode of criticism inherited from Spain which stresses form over content, "a criticism that enjoys counting and appreciating adjectives, enumerating and classifying metaphors—above all if they show synesthesia—recounting to infinity what has been said from Alfonso the Sage to the present, without taking into account that times and people and societies change or are different in different countries" ("Some Ideas about Criticism," 235). Laguerre feels impelled to break his rule of not commenting upon criticism of his work in protesting a Marxist interpretation of *The Fingers of the Hand* which appeared in *Asomante,* and insists that socialism there forms the historical background against which he examines individual conduct in itself and as a reflection of social conduct, but without any dogmatism.

Laguerre's literary preferences lead him away from writers most concerned with artistic form like Góngora and Darío ("About Language") and toward Jorge Manrique, Bécquer, and above all Antonio Machado, for whom language is a vehicle of profound expression. He has no patience with "the sterility of pure intellectualism" that does not lead to any social achievement ("Puerto Rican Theater of the Present," 299). As for language in Puerto Rico, Laguerre feels that it is no worse off than anywhere else and praises the island's capacity to Hispanize English words and adapt them into Spanish in a dynamic fashion. He maintains a moderate position regarding purism or changes, suggesting the compilation of a dictionary of Hispanic-American Spanish and the establishment of a linguistic commission to standardize Puerto Rican Spanish in view of its own social and communicative needs. The prose style of these essays is neat and unaffected, clearly a vehicle for effective communication. Metaphors are few and only used for graphic comparison inspired by nature. He speaks of a critic "who lives tied to old formulas like the burr to the hem of the pants" (239) and of the characters portrayed by Arriví's play *Bachelors' Club* as male *quenepos* (a type of native tree) which promise to bear fruit each spring but never do, since the male *quenepo* cannot produce fruit.

Perhaps what is most fascinating for the present-day reader of these essays created in the early 1950s is to note that so many of Laguerre's suggestions have been implemented. Cultural competitions and festivals, the restoration of Old San Juan as a museum-park, greater diffusion of Puerto Rican literature, the eradication of illiteracy, official sponsorship of cultural and artistic projects, and increased educational opportunities have fulfilled many, though certainly not all, of his foresighted recommendations voiced as a public service on the radio.

Polos de la cultura iberoamericana [Poles of Ibero-American Culture] is a collection of lectures, articles, reviews, and general essays inspired by the "poles" of Spanish revisionist thought of the Generation of '98 introduced in Puerto Rico by Antonio S. Pedreira and native Ibero-Americanism promoted by Concha Meléndez, to whom the volume is dedicated.[14] The topics treated flow from general Ibero-American themes to Puerto Rico, the Antilles, Mexico, and Brazil. We find commentary on the poetry of Luis Lloréns Torres and on language in Puerto Rico and Spanish America, a penetrating study of "Women in the Tragedies of Gertrudis Gómez de Avellaneda," and a comparative study of "Two Visions of Hell" in the Brazilian writer Graciliano Ramos's *Vidas sêcas* and the Mexican novelist Juan Rulfo's *Pedro Páramo*. Laguerre also dedicates essays to contemporary cultural heroes of Puerto Rico instrumental in forging national consciousness, such as Concha Meléndez, Francisco Manrique Cabrera, Vicente Géigel Polanco, and Margot Arce de Vázquez, as well as to Spaniards in Puerto Rico, the educator Federico de Onís and the sculptor Compostela, mentioned in *The Labyrinth*. The concept of Ibero-Americanism is present in his discussions of the Antilleanism in Hostos and Martí, the "magna homeland" idea of Pedro Henríquez Ureña, and Brazilian literature as part of a common American culture. In a tribute to the Mexican critic and professor Andrés Iduarte, Laguerre tells of the latter's advice to him to change his address after writing *The Labyrinth* because its controversial subject endangered his life, a warning which evidently was well founded, according to the author.

Several essays are particularly interesting in that they provide valuable indications of Laguerre's motives and inspiration in writing fiction. Since he is usually reticent about self-commentary, these are rare opportunities to learn what he esteems most in his novels. In the first essay of the volume, for example, he acknowledges his debt to Concha Meléndez, who opened his eyes to the concept of Puerto Rico as part of

Ibero-America in times of great cultural confusion generated both by the "Americanization" program, which aspired to impose the language and mores of the United States, and by nostalgia for the Spanish mother country.

"Leavening of History in Puerto Rican Narrative" may be considered an organic essay in explaining Laguerre's consistent use of myth in his novels, which he calls the "religion of nationality" and a need that exists even in the most pragmatic countries. He also clarifies once and for all his political posture, repudiating the type of independence inspired by a return to the traditions of Spain combated in the last scene of *The Undertow,* and that which espouses international Marxism; he accepts only the idea of independence nourished by the Puerto Rican's particular mode of life and social and spiritual conduct. "I don't think it wise to decide upon an internationalist independence before we have complete conscience of our national identity or integrity" (59). Laguerre also defends his faith in the concept of "Indafrispanism," explained by Adalberto Linares in the novel *Fire and Its Air,* not just as a synthesis of racial shades but "national conscience fermented by noble fantasy in the holiest trinity of land (nature), fire (passion) and air (breath)" (61–62). As a national novelist he examines the questions of what am I and what do I want to be, using concrete realities, among them "fantasy, the most exalted of human realities" (61). He notes that from his earliest works he alternates indigenous and African myths with Greco-Latin ones, using nature as primary mythical inspiration. He considers his protagonists' explorations into the soul of national life and many characters as mythical transfigurations of Puerto Rican history. He points to the type of reader response he most appreciates in the example of a young lady who exclaimed that she was in love with Dolorito Montojo, having taken him from the fictional world of *The Undertow* into the real world of her sentiments and of Puerto Rican life.

Further insights into Laguerre's attitudes are revealed in "Contemporary Puerto Rican Literature," inspired by three satires by Luis Rechani Agrait about those who deny their own cultural heritage. Recalling the contributions of the Generation of 1930, influenced by the spirit of renovation of the Spanish Generation of '98 and by Ibero-Americanism, he notes the flowering of Puerto Rican culture in all the arts even with the difficulties in achieving international recognition and the support of periodicals. He denies that the North American presence in Puerto Rico has paralyzed native culture; on the contrary, the intensified need for cultural affirmation has stimulated "more and better cultivators of the arts" (73). It is clear that Laguerre is concerned with a moral attitude rather than any political stance:

> As a matter of fact, many are those with nationalistic sentiments who are, paradoxically, in favor of statehood for Puerto Rico. They say they want to conserve language, customs, traditions, and nevertheless defend federated statehood. On the other hand, there are independence advocates who have submitted to North American acculturation . . . I am of the opinion that our writers ought to commit themselves to the idea of preserving Puerto Rican identity. (66)

A final statement of social and pedagogical philosophy may be found in "The Responsibility of the University Professor," decrying elitism, evasion, and exclusiveness of specialization. With reference to literature, Laguerre sees it primarily as communication and views works of the past in their enrichment of the present. "It is good, let us say, to study Góngora, but without wasting the better part of life trying to find out the sense of one or another sentence with significance more circumstantial than permanent" (75–76). He cites the university's responsibilities of preserving and amplifying knowledge, cleansing it of superstition and political, religious, and ideological fanaticism, training professionals for serving the nation, anticipating programs for progress, stimulating investigation, and responding creatively to social needs. With the same sense of tolerance we find in his novels, he states: "One may have a certain religious, political preference and favor a certain government without falling into moral servitude" (81). Any who would interpret Laguerre's work as politically inspired would certainly have to heed these words.

Laguerre has written numerous prologues for anthologies and works by other authors. One of the most fascinating of these is in his 1978 edition of *La charca* [The Mud Pool, 1894] by Manuel Zeno Gandía, which, in addition to the forty-page prologue, includes a hundred pages of chronology, setting the author's life against cultural, historical, political, and scientific events in Puerto Rico, Latin America, and the international scene.[15] Laguerre insists on the importance of relating the life of Zeno Gandía to his times and in doing so reveals a prodigious knowledge of world culture and an ability to relate diverse and copious data. While he dedicates these pages to an in-depth critical evaluation of the author studied, he cannot help but express his own ideas about writing novels, so that his comments constitute a veritable elucidation of his literary philosophy without detracting in any way from the object of his study.

Two major aspects may be distinguished in Laguerre's discussion of Zeno Gandía, biographical and literary, though they do not appear separately in the prologue. It is clear that the critic does not admire the novelist's European, aristocratic, conservative, and traditional inclinations. He finds more intellectual interest in social problems than real social concern, thus weakening the ideological focus. For Laguerre, Zeno Gandía fails to denounce colonial abuses with an eye to reform and instead blames collective indifference, which he attributes to tropical environment and racial mixture in a Naturalistic determinism imposed by the author. The critic nevertheless recognizes the value of Zeno Gandía's "Chronicles of a Sick World" in calling attention to the desperate social situation which existed in a difficult moment of Puerto Rican history, the last decade of the nineteenth century and the first decades of the twentieth, awakening the social consciousness of subsequent generations, including that of Laguerre. He respects the novelist's intentions to contribute to social criticism and his love for Puerto Rico.

In discussing Zeno Gandía's artistic treatment, Laguerre applauds the poetical qualities of his descriptions of nature, even when these descriptions constitute a motive of evasion. His most severe criticism is reserved for the novelist's treatment of character, which is of capital importance to Laguerre: "The most outstanding works of world literary creation have stood out precisely for their refined and complex characterization" (xxxv). "The drama is not in causes but in effects. One puts the characters into motion, judges them from the greatest number of angles to go in search of their integral conduct. They must not be simply 'good' or 'bad' but like the people one sees everywhere, some simpler and others more complex" (xxxv–vi). The critic enunciates ideas on the novel which undoubtedly have influenced his own inventions:

> No matter how real a novel tries to be, in truth it is not real life. Without the element of fiction and synthesis one cannot include everything in a determined number of pages. . . . We have never believed—time is proving us right—that more importance should be given to the innovation of techniques or formulas of the genre than to the creation of characters and the dramatization of ideas. (xxxvi)

He says that the novel is a vehicle of entertainment and of reflection and cites as models *Madame Bovary, The Trial* (Kafka), *Moby-Dick,* the *Quijote, The Brothers Karamazov, Ulysses,* and *In Search of Lost Time* (Proust). He criticizes in Zeno Gandía the direct intervention of the author in judging characters, the repetition of certain types, characters who are merely spokesmen of the author, and insufficient infusion of fantasy and invention into real events, although these defects vary in different works. This prologue, then, is invaluable as a statement of novelistic philosophy and as a recognition of fundamental differences between Laguerre and his predecessor as a novelist of social concerns, Zeno Gandía.

In a discussion of Laguerre's essays, a final word must be given to the underlying attitude of disinterested publice service which inspires his weekly column "Free Pages," published in the newspaper *El Mundo* since 1959. He accepted the project under two conditions, that not even a comma be changed and that he not be paid. In the hundreds of columns commenting upon local and international events, he has been an implacable defender of many of the principles which inform his novels, such as the conservation of Puerto Rico's natural beauty and resources, which made him a precursor of ecologists, and the denunciation of false and superficial values. He has consistently maintained an attitude of independent criteria and avoided involvement in partisanships or vested interests in these journalistic essays, which have no other purpose than to voice his concerns as a responsible writer and citizen.

Chapter Ten
Summary and Conclusions

Enrique A. Laguerre's writings have followed changing experiences of the Puerto Rican on his journey through the twentieth century, novelizing his problems and conflicts and examining his identity as a Puerto Rican and as an inhabitant of the world, as an individual and as part of society. The major trends of Latin American fiction during the past half-century are discernible in his novels, where regionalism, social protest, and magical realism do not form separate periods but rather the subsoil of his artistic creation from his earliest works to the most recent ones, although the emphasis on one and another may vary.

Dimensions of Human Experience

The aspects of man's experience which interest Laguerre are fundamentally those which are moral, psychological, and social. There is a definite commitment to the search for lasting and authentic values, inviting a continual reexamination of self in the context of individual and collective conduct. It is not difficult to perceive the author's essential faith in humankind; few of his characters are all bad, like the tyrant in *The Labyrinth* and Pasamonte in *The Undertow,* though in the latter upbringing is largely to blame. The underlying belief that education and the examination of conscience can help to correct the evils of the individual, who collectively forms society, makes his fiction a statement of optimism in spite of the fact that happy endings are extremely rare (*The Ceiba Tree in the Flower Pot).* Laguerre seems to imply that individual action may not be able to change the world but that each person, however humble, can contribute, within the range of his own little spot on the globe—be it a minuscule fishing village, a mountain plantation, or an island in the Caribbean—to make it a better place to live. The question of why innocent people suffer is a reiterated disquieting note to be found in all his novels, and of course, remains unanswered. While physical hunger and illness are definite concerns, perhaps more important is spiritual hunger which many Laguerrean protagonists experience in a society where spiritual illness abounds, where materialism and the cult of power conspire against higher values. We would not call Laguerre a moralist because he does not preach or propose a program of regeneration; he does, however, portray a moral climate in which his characters struggle to find values.

The "heroes" of Laguerre's fictions are often at odds with themselves, in conflict between what they are and what they want to be or feel they should have been. Many of them, as critics have noted, at one time or another in their harried lives contemplate suicide. Yet, and this is very significant, they carry on without yielding to suicide. They are psychologically credible in terms of their experience and environment but do not respond to a Naturalistic or deterministic view of life, since, as we have indicated, the possibility of regeneration is ever present, though not always taken. Many of them suffer from the same existential loneliness, alienation, and confusion that appear in almost all the literature of our times. Laguerre's protagonists are frequently orphaned of one or both parents, which suggests existential connotations. In *The 30th of February,* this alienation is existential and metaphysical; in other novels it is associated with Puerto Rican circumstances, such as the encroachment of a foreign (American) life-style, hostile environment such as that of New York, lack of a clear life project related to indecision in the island's political status and destiny, or conflicts of conscience resulting from living a life devoid of authentic and traditional values. Images of suffocation and entrapment help to underscore these feelings, hence the symbolism accorded the labyrinth, fish net, spider web, tiny flower pot, and fire without air. Nature, particularly that of the mountains, consistently has positive connotations in Laguerre's fictions, in contrast to the constricting effects of urban civilization and its demands.

Social themes characterize our author's writings from the inception of his literary career, for he is sensitive to the plight of oppressed woman, children, and workers. His most exemplary female characters are usually social workers or teachers *(The Blaze, Montoya Plantation, River Bed without a River).* Laguerre's early protagonists tend to be or imagine themselves to be victims of injustice or frustrated reformers, but in

River Bed without a River, Fire and Its Air, and *Benevolent Masters* characters who are affluent, powerful, and supposedly successful react to the emptiness of their lives. There is a constant striving for social equality, awareness, and justice implicit in these fictions. The emphasis on individual protagonists, though they may retreat from view to permit the reader to observe others, reminds us that individual responsibility is at the core of all Laguerre's social themes.

History, Myth, and Fable

Laguerre is inspired by the generation of 1930s' aspiration to instil historical consciousness in the Puerto Rican. He gives special attention to the expression of legends, folklore, myths, fables, and traditions, not to celebrate the past as an end in itself but to enrich the present and give meaning and continuity to the future. Some myths glorified in the novels are taken from Puerto Rican traditions of Taíno heroes and gods (*The Ceiba Tree in the Flower Pot, The Undertow, Fire and Its Air*), but frequently biblical and classical sources provide symbolism and allusions. These become increasingly universal in the later novels, and African, Egyptian, and even extraterrestrial in *Benevolent Masters*. Laguerre employs mythification to elevate characters and events to heroic stature and demythification to disclose irony. These myths and legends add a dimension of timelessness to the novels and also impart lyrical qualities when used as leitmotifs. They begin as stories of superstition and legend inserted in *Montoya Plantation* and end up flowing throughout the novels, providing lyricism and magical realism, which in Laguerre may be more exactly called mysterious realism, since there is more mystery than magic.

Laguerre's novels and his play are situated against a historical backdrop which seen as a block traces the history of Puerto Rico from the last decades of the nineteenth century to the 1970s. In Laguerre literary fabulation joins the legends and fables of the popular imagination to complement history and make it live.

Artistic Characteristics of His Inventions

One of Laguerre's favored artistic devices is the metaphor, appearing singly or in related groups and reiterated as leitmotifs. They are present in all the titles of his novels except *Montoya Plantation*. Titles are evidently arrived at after great meditation in order to capture the essence of the novels in a poetical way. Situation often assumes metaphorical value and proper names frequently contain or suggest symbolism or metaphors. Laguerre's prose is also capable of great lyricism, particularly when inspired by the natural beauty of Puerto Rico.

Characters and settings, such as Los Robles and Río Loco, recur in several novels, creating one unified novelistic world which is, of course, a facsimile of Puerto Rico. In fact all of Laguerre's novels and stories may be considered as sequels of one another since they follow the development and history of Puerto Rico and form what may be considered a single body of fiction. The imaginative world of Laguerre's novels is not always distinct from the real world. Many characters and places are, by the author's own confession, taken from reality. In fact some people have been able to recognize themselves in his novels and have even called themselves by their fictional name. Real places are sometimes called by their real names (Río Loco, for example) or are disguised by fictional names, such as in *The Undertow,* where the El Yunque rain forest becomes the Yukiyú and the River Mameyes the River Espejo (Mirror) because of its bright, clear waters. The house of the Moreau family of *The Blaze* outside of Aguadillas has been restored by the Institute of Puerto Rican Culture and is the site of cultural and academic excursions. It may be said in truth that the reality of Laguerre's novels has transcended the transitory existence of the original models, which, "leavened" by imagination, continue to live in the pages of his fictions. Well-known people appear as occasional characters in *Fire and Its Air* and characters step out of the pages of the book to provide epigraphs and even to be the object of the author's initial personal dedication in *River Bed without a River.* Laguerre's first novel becomes a subject of discussion in his second one, causing a profound impression on its fictitious reader.

Laguerre uses a variety of original structures, transversal in *The Blaze;* bipartite in *Montoya Plantation, River Bed without a River,* and *The Labyrinth;* and interchangeable in *Benevolent Masters.* He handles slow pace (the first part of *Montoya Plantation,* for example) and action scenes (in *The Undertow*) equally well. Potentially scatological scenes in *The Labyrinth, The Undertow,* and *Fire and Its Air* are treated with frankness but at the same time with notable decorum. Irony is abundant in Laguerre's fiction, where it is both linguistic and situational.

The Blaze and *The Ceiba Tree in the Flower Pot* are narrated in the first person and the illusion of first-person expression is given by increasing use of interior monologue. This becomes more complicated as multiple interior monologue with a sliding point of view is expertly handled in *Fire and Its Air* and with exceptional ease in *Benevolent Masters*. Linguistic experimentation and innovation are present in *Fire and Its Air,* but generally Laguerre is careful not to let virtuosity of style detract from content.

In conclusion, it may be said that Enrique A. Laguerre's most significant artistic accomplishment is that of creating in his fiction a saga of a land and its people, but at the same time his vision transcends geographical contexts and projects his novels into the timeless and universal relevance of all great art.

Notes and References

Chapter One

1. Much of the geo-historical information in this chapter may be found in José A. Toro Sugrañes, *Almanaque boricua* (San Juan: Editorial Cordillera, 1978). Biographical data have been compiled from Josefina Rivera de Álverez, *Diccionario de la literatura puertorriqueña,* Tomo Segundo, Volumen II (San Juan, 1974), pp. 812–13; Luis O. Zayas Micheli's book, cited below; and letters from the author and conversations with him.
2. Concha Meléndez, *La generación del treinta: Cuento y novela* (San Juan: Instituto de Cultura Puertorriqueña, 1972), publication of a lecture given April 11, 1958.
3. Luis O. Zayas Micheli, *Lo universal en Enrique A. Laguerre* (Río Piedras: Editorial Edil, 1974), pp. 47–48.
4. Antonio S. Pedreira's prologue to the second edition of Laguerre's *La llamarada,* dated 1937, and found in subsequent editions of the individual work (Mexico: Ediciones Orión, 1961), p. 10.
5. Fernando Alegría, *Historia de la novela hispanoamericana,* 3rd ed. (Mexico: Andrea, 1966), p. 208.
6. The late arrival of literary movements is noted repeatedly in *Literatura puertorriqueña: 21 conferencias* (San Juan: Instituto de Cultura Puertorriqueña, 1969) in Julia María Guzmán's "Realismo y naturalismo en Puerto Rico," pp. 150–51; Adriana Ramos Mimoso's "El modernismo en la lírica puertorriqueña," p. 102; and Modesto Rivera's "El modernismo.—La prosa," pp. 214–15.

Chapter Two

1. *Historia de la novela hispanoamericana,* 3rd ed., p. 173.
2. Ibid., pp. 173, 205–209. Here Alegría notes such changes.
3. "Prólogo a la segunda edición" (1937), in *La llamarada,* 17th ed. (Barcelona: Ediciones Rumbos, 1968), p. 6.
4. *Lo universal en Enrique A. Laguerre* (Río Piedras, 1974), p. 131; Zayas refers to Manuel Zeno Gandía's naturalistic novel of 1894, considered a milestone in Puerto Rican fiction.
5. *Obras completas* (San Juan, 1974), I: pages cited in parentheses are from this edition.

6. *El fuego y su aire* (Buenos Aires, 1970), p. 126.
7. *Meditaciones del Quijote e ideas sobre la novela*, 5th ed. (Madrid: Revista de Occidente, 1958), p. 177.
8. See *Insularismo, ensayos de interpretación puertorriqueña* (Madrid: Tip. Artística, 1934).
9. The poem is reproduced in Francisco Manrique Cabrera, *Historia de la literatura puertorriqueña* (New York: Las Américas Pub. Co., 1956), p. 57. Island sugar cultivation is present in a lesser degree in the background of Zeno Gandía's 1896 novel *Garduña: Chronicle of a Sick World*.
10. In Cesáreo Rosa-Nieves, *Aguinaldo lírico de la poesía puertorriqueña* (Río Piedras:Editorial Edil, 1971), I, 371–75.
11. Ibid., III, 162–63.
12. *La generación del treinta: Cuento y novela*, p. 31.

Chapter Three

1. Prologue to *Solar Montoya*, in Enrique A. Laguerre, *Obras completas* (San Juan, 1974), I, 239.
2. Ibid.
3. Enrique A. Laguerre and Esther M. Melón, *El jíbaro de Puerto Rico: símbolo y figura* (Sharon, Conn., 1968), p. xii. A selection from Antonio A. Pedreira's essay "La actualidad del jíbaro," which establishes two jíbaro cycles, is included in this volume, pp. 7–24.
4. *El jíbaro*, p. xii.
5. *Obras completas*, I: pages in parentheses in the text.
6. *Historia de la literatura puertorriqueña*, p. 101.
7. See *Lo universal en Enrique A. Laguerre*, pp. 90–109.
8. *Imagen del puertorriqueño en la novela* (Río Piedras, 1976), p. 86.
9. Zayas Micheli, p. 104.

Chapter Four

1. *Obras completas*, I: pages cited in this section are from this edition.
2. Concha Meléndez and Luis O. Zayas Micheli in books cited below and Josefina Rivera de Álvarez, *Diccionario de la literatura puertorriqueña*, II, 814.
3. Concha Meléndez, *La generación del treinta*, p. 33; Zayas Micheli, *Lo universal en Enrique A. Laguerre*, p. 163.
4. *Obras completas*, II: pages in parentheses.
5. *Imagen del puertorriqueño en la novela*, p. 129. Beauchamp mentions that the nickname is significant.
6. Zayas Micheli, p. 230.

Chapter Five

1. Angelina Morfi, *Enrique A. Laguerre y su obra . . . "La resaca," cumbre en su arte de novelar* (San Juan 1964), pp. 76–79. Among critics cited are Concha Meléndez, Francisco Manrique Cabrera, Luis Hernández Aquino, Josefina Guevara Casteñeira, Enrique Anderson-Imbert, Andrés Iduarte.
2. Ibid., pp. 79–80.
3. Enrique A. Laguerre, *Obras completas* (San Juan, 1974), II: pages are cited in parentheses.
4. Concha Meléndez, *"La resaca," Obras completas* (San Juan, 1970), II, 414.
5. Francisco Manrique Cabrera does not consider it a true national episode since the historical part serves only as background. ("Notas sobre la novela puertorriqueña de los últimos veinticinco años," *Asomante* [1935]: 25). The Unamunian term "intrahistory" may best describe the novel, communicating history in an individual life, in the small things which reflect the epoch. In any case the "bio" part of bionovel can refer to the life of one person or to that of a people in an important moment of its history.
6. Information on Lares may be found in all books which treat nineteenth-century history of Puerto Rico. An especially good source is the issue of *Revista del Instituto de Cultura Puertorriqueña* (San Juan) 40 (July–September 1968), dedicated to the Lares centenary.
7. "Los tiempos del gobernador Sanz," *Pulso de Puerto Rico, 1952–1954* (San Juan, 1956), p. 121.
8. "Un libro de Antonio Rivera," *Pulso de Puerto Rico,* p. 126.
9. Ibid., p. 127. Laguerre cites this as Rivera's thesis. This view, of the autonomy offer, sustained by many historians, also appears in Del Rosario, Melón de Díaz, Martinez Masdeu, *Breve enciclopedia de la cultura puertorriqueña* (San Juan: Editorial Cordillera 1976), p. 231.
10. *Pulso de Puerto Rico*, p. 119.
11. Luis O. Zayas Micheli, *Lo universal en Enrique A. Laguerre,* p. 194.
12. Concha Meléndez, p. 109. No specific political situation is offered; Dr. Meléndez extracts the most essential aspects here.
13. Laguerre, *La poesía modernista en Puerto Rico* (San Juan, 1969), p. 18.
14. Ibid., p. 35.
15. Concha Meléndez, p. 409.
16. "Leavening of History in Puerto Rican Narrative," *Polos de la cultura iberoamericana* (Boston, 1977), pp. 57–64; *Pulso de Puerto Rico,* p. 138.
17. Don Quijote is amply cited by José Juan Beauchamp *(Imagen del puertorriqueño en la novela),* Morfi, and Zayas with regard to the frustrated hero. While there is some reminiscence of Cervantes's master creation—

chastity, ideal love, some successful adventures and others unsuccessful—there is not a great deal of reliance on this model for the creation of Dolorito. In fact, in one scene, p. 154, Balbino acts like an exalted Quijote, and Salú, his henchman, like a proverb-spouting Sancho. In view of the struggle for autonomy from Spain which appears in the novel *The Undertow,* it would seem counterproductive to adhere to a Spanish model, even though it is a masterpiece.

18. Laguerre praises Cordero in his essay "La educación como niveladora social" [Education as a Social Leveler], *Pulso de Puerto Rico,* p. 164. See also Eugenio Fernández Méndez, *Viaje histórico de un pueblo,* p. 139. Ironically, Cordero died the same year as the Cry of Lares, in 1868.

19. José Hernández, *Martín Fierro,* ed. Estelle Irizarry (Zaragoza: Editorial Ebro, 1975), pp. 207–209. Verses cited are 2311–12 and 2351–54.

Chapter Six

1. *Obras completas,* II: pages cited in parentheses.

2. Arriví, *"La ceiba en el tiesto.* Entrada por las raíces," *El Mundo* (San Juan), October 20, 1956, p. 14; Marqués, *"La ceiba en el tiesto.* La novela de Laguerre en nuestra literatura actual," *El Mundo,* May 26, 1956, p. 22; Meléndez, *La generación del treinta,* p. 35; Beauchamp, *Imagen del puertorriqueño en la novela,* p. 137; Zayas, *Lo universal en Enrique A. Laguerre,* p. 335.

3. Eugenio Fernández Méndez, *Viaje histórico de un pueblo,* pp. 239–46. References to this period may be found in Laguerre's book of essays *Pulso de Puerto Rico, 1952–1954.*

4. Beauchamp, p. 138, referring to Navarro Tomás, *"La ceiba en el tiesto," El Mundo,* July 7, 1956, p. 20.

5. Beauchamp, p. 153.

6. F. Manrique Cabrera, *Historia de la literatura puertorriqueña,* p. 223.

7. José Emilio González calls it "one of the best novels of Laguerre, probably one of the best of our literature" in *"La ceiba en el tiesto," Asomante* (San Juan) 16 (October–December 1956): 110; for Meléndez (p. 35) it is "the novel in which the artistic intentions of the author are realized with the most appropriate balance."

8. *The Labyrinth,* translated by William Rose (New York, 1960), pages indicated in parentheses. José Juan Beauchamp, pp. 91–92.

9. Thomas Bulfinch, *Bulfinch's Mythology* (New York: Avenel, 1978), p. 152.

10. Russell R. Fitzgibbon, "Editor's Preface" to Jesús de Galíndez's *The Era of Trujillo* (Tucson: University of Arizona Press, 1973), pp. xi–xviii.

11. Arturo R. Espaillat, *Trujillo: The Last Caesar* (Chicago: Henry Regnery Co., 1963), p. 112.
12. Ibid., p. 13.
13. Galíndez, p. 202.

Chapter Seven

1. *Cauce sin río* (San Juan, 1962), pages in parentheses.
2. *Pulso de Puerto Rico,* pp. 263, 303.
3. The quotation is from Job III: 16. Other passages from the same book are suggested on another occasion when Víctor recalls how he *"met with darkness and groped in the dark as in the night. Stranger I was to the eyes of my best friends"* (33).
4. *Lo universal en Enrique A. Laguerre,* pp. 374–75.
5. Rubén del Rosario, Esther Melón de Díaz, Edgar Martínez Masdeu, *Breve enciclopedia de la cultura puertorriqueña,* p. 243.
6. This irony is perceptively noted by Juan Martínez Capó, "La escena literaria," *Puerto Rico Ilustrado* (Supplement of *El Mundo*), August 15, 1971, p. 18.
7. The theme of identity is commented upon by José Emilio González, "El fuego y su aire," *Sin Nombre* (San Juan) 1 (1971): 96–97; Concha Meléndez, *Literatura de ficción en Puerto Rico,* p. 190. Zayas Micheli defines the alleged identity dilemma as that of integration of a fragmented personality, p. 393.
8. Martínez Capó, p. 18; Zayas, p. 392.
9. *El fuego y su aire* (Buenos Aires, 1970), pages in parentheses.
10. Martínez Capó, p. 18.
11. Zayas (p. 391) quotes "Citas y críticas de *El fuego y su aire,*" *El Mundo,* December 9, 1971, in which Laguerre discovers in some of his ideas and those of the English writer R. D. Laing and the German novelist Günter Grass surprising coincidences which he attributes to the times.

Chapter Eight

1. *Aspects of the Novel* (New York: 1954), pp. 53 and 49, respectively.
2. *Los amos benévolos* (Río Piedras, 1977). Pages indicated in parentheses are from this edition. Translations are by Gino Parisi from the forthcoming English edition to be published by the Instituto de Cultura Puertorriqueña, San Juan.
3. *El Mundo* (San Juan), June 3, 1979, p. 12B.

4. "El pensamiento mítico en *Los amos benévolos,*" *Horizontes* (Ponce, Puerto Rico) 38 (1976): 63–66.
5. "Prólogo a la segunda edición," dated 1937, in *La llamarada,* 17th ed. (Barcelona, 1968), p.6.
6. *Obras completas,* I, 61, 162.

Chapter Nine

1. Francisco Arriví, "La generación del treinta: El teatro," *Literatura puertorriqueña: 21 conferencias,* p. 379.
2. Arriví, *Areyto mayor* (San Juan, 1966), p. 55; see also Emilio J. Pasarell, *Orígenes y desarrollo de la afición teatral en Puerto Rico–Siglo XX* Editorial Universitaria, (Río Piedras: 1967), II, 181–82.
3. Laguerre, *La resentida* (Barcelona, 1960), pages in parentheses.
4. Laguerre notes that the dense symbolism in Arriví's theater sometimes obscures his intentions, making it difficult to perceive the message, in "El teatro puertorriqueño del presente," *Pulso de Puerto Rico,* p. 299.
5. Arriví in *La generación del treinta,* p. 392, and *Areyto mayor,* p. 56; Zayas Micheli in *Lo universal en Enrique A. Laguerre,* p. 57; Josefina Álvarez de Rivera, *Diccionario de la literatura puertorriqueña,* II, 181–82.
6. Laguerre and Melón, *El jíbaro en Puerto Rico,* pages in parentheses.
7. Ibid., p. 198.
8. Meléndez, *El arte del cuento en Puerto Rico* (New York, 1961), pages in parentheses.
9. Published in ibid., pp. 128–36.
10. Morfi, *Enrique A. Laguerre y su obra "La resaca," cumbre en su arte de novelar,* p. 53.
11. *La poesía modernista en Puerto Rico* (San Juan, 1969), pages in parentheses.
12. *Pulso de Puerto Rico* (San Juan, 1956), pages and individual essay titles in parentheses.
13. *El fuego y su aire,* p. 126.
14. *Polos de la cultura iberoamericana* (Boston, 1977), pages in parentheses.
15. *La charca* (Caracas, 1978), pages in parentheses.

Selected Bibliography

PRIMARY SOURCES

Listed below are Laguerre's writings which have been published as books or incorporated into books.

1. Novels (since most of Laguerre's novels have appeared in several editions, only the first edition is listed)

Los amos benévolos. Río Piedras: Universidad de Puerto Rico, Editorial Universitaria, 1977.

Benevolent Masters. San Juan: Instituto de Cultura Puertorriqueña, in press. Translation by Gino Parisi.

Cauce sin río. Madrid: Nuevas Editoriales Unidas, 1962.

La ceiba en el tiesto. San Juan: Biblioteca de Autores Puertorriqueños, 1956.

Los dedos de la mano. San Juan: Biblioteca de Autores Puertorriqueños, 1951.

El fuego y su aire. Buenos Aires: Losada, 1970.

El laberinto. New York: Las Américas, 1959.

The Labyrinth, New York: Las Américas, 1960. Translation by William Rose.

La llamarada. Aguadilla, P. R. : Tipografía Fidel Ruiz, 1935. (Twenty-three editions have been published as of December 1979.)

La resaca (Bionovela). San Juan: Biblioteca de Autores Puertorriqueños, 1949.

Solar Montoya. San Juan: Imprenta Venezuela, 1941.

El 30 de febrero. Vida de un hombre interino. San Juan: Biblioteca de Autores Puertorriqueños, 1943.

2. Complete Works (most recent edition)

Obras completas. San Juan: Instituto de Cultura Puertorriqueña, 1974. Volume I includes *La llamarada, Solar Montoya, El 30 de febrero.* Volume II includes: *La resaca, Los dedos de la mano, La ceiba en el tiesto.*

3. Theater

La resentida. Barcelona: Ediciones Rumbos, 1960.

4. Essays and Prologues Mentioned in This Study

El jíbaro de Puerto Rico: Símbolo y figura (in collaboration with Esther M. Melón). Sharon, Conn.: Troutman Press, 1968. Introduction and comments preceding each section of the anthology.

La poesía modernista en Puerto Rico. San Juan: Editorial Coquí, 1969.

Polos de la cultura iberoamericana. Boston: Florentia Publishers, 1977.

"Prólogo y cronología," Manuel Zeno Gandía's *La charca*. Caracas: Biblioteca Ayacucho, 1978.

Pulso de Puerto Rico, 1952–1954. San Juan: Biblioteca de Autores Puertorriqueños, 1956.

5. Short Stories

"El enemigo." In Concha Meléndez, *El Arte del cuento en Puerto Rico*. New York: Las Américas, 1961, pp. 137–43.

"Naufragio." In ibid., pp. 128–36.

"Pacholí." In Laguerre and Melón, *El jíbaro de Puerto Rico*, pp. 193–98.

"Raíces." In ibid., pp. 185–92; Concha Meléndez, pp. 120–27; Laguerre, *Antología de cuentos puertorriqueños*, Mexico: Editorial Orión, 1955, pp. 147–56; Cesáreo Rosa-Nieves, *El costumbrismo literario en la prosa de Puerto Rico*, Vol. II. San Juan: Cordillera, 1971, pp. 167–77.

SECONDARY SOURCES

1. Books

Beauchamp, José Juan. *Imagen del puertorriqueño en la novela (En Alejandro Tapia y Rivera, Manuel Zeno Gandía y Enrique A. Laguerre)*. Río Piedras: Editorial Universitaria, Universidad de Puerto Rico, 1976. Treats the jíbaro, the Negro and the emigrant, collective and representative characters, and the use of metaphors, images, and symbols in Laguerre's novels in pp. 71–160. Well-organized study which, despite the expected brevity, provides excellent insights. Bibliography of ninety entries.

Casanova Sánchez, Olga. *La crítica social en la obra novelística de Enrique A. Laguerre*. Río Piedras: Editorial Cultural, 1975. Less than half the book is actually about the jíbaro, the land, influence of the United States, politics, and the Puerto Rican in New York as portrayed in Laguerre's novels. The first four chapters treat the history of Puerto Rico, social themes in its literature, the novel before Laguerre, and the latter's life and works. Useful as a thematic overview.

García Cabrera, Manuel. *Laguerre y sus polos de la cultura iberoamericana*. San Juan: Biblioteca de Autores Puertorriqueños, 1978. A useful guide to the reading of Laguerre's book of essays *Polos de la cultura iberoamericana*, a sort of running commentary and summary with excerpts from a personal point of view of a contemporary of Laguerre who is editor of the Biblioteca de Autores Puertorriqueños, which published many first editions of Laguerre's novels and other important works of Puerto Rico.

Monserrat, María del Carmen. *La personalidad del puertorriqueño en dos novelas de autores de Puerto Rico (aspectos educativos)*. San Juan: Instituto de Cultura Puertorriqueña, in press. Treats *Benevolent Masters*. An extensive, well-researched biography and a bibliography of some 1,700 entries make this a valuable resource book.

Morfi, Angelina. *Enrique A. Laguerre y su obra "La resaca," cumbre en su arte de novelar*. San Juan: Instituto de Cultura Puertorriqueña, 1964. Originally a master's thesis, the book treats Puerto Rican history and literature, Laguerre's biography and novels to 1962. Covers *The Undertow's* primary and secondary themes, structure, and characters. The major part of the book studies lexicon, adjectivation, images and symbols, verbs and syntax, classical figures of speech, in a primarily preceptive approach. Good bibliography.

Rosa-Nieves, Cesáreo. *Cañas al sol en "La llamarada."* Humacao: Tipografía Comercial, 1938. A thirteen-page pamphlet, one of the first analyses of *The Blaze*, it studies the fusion of nature, man, and beast, and social attitudes, with good comments about metaphor and the use of color in Laguerre's "novelized poem of man and land."

Zayas Micheli, Luis O. *Lo universal en Enrique A. Laguerre (Estudio conjunto de su obra)*. Río Piedras: Editorial Edil, 1974. This revision of the author's Ph.D. thesis tries to be all encompassing, including Puerto Rican history, the novel in Puerto Rico, biography of Laguerre, his humor, use of Anglicisms, methods of interiorization of reality, etc. Most valuable in its study of the psychology of protagonists. Divides novels into National and International Cycles and treats universality mainly stemming from national considerations, namely the extent to which Laguerre anticipates theories of Albert Memmi and Frantz Fanon about the effects of colonization, with occasional references to other contemporary thinkers. Very brief bibliography.

2. Articles (a brief selection based on extension and profundity, with special regard for accessibility for the general reader)

Arriví, Francisco. "Segundo festival de teatro puertorriqueño 1959." In *Areyto mayor*. San Juan: Instituto de Cultura Puertorriqueña, 1966, pp.

24, 55–56. Gives background on the development of the Puerto Rican theater and provides an interesting description of the author's preparation for writing *The Resentful Woman* and the actual staging.

Cabrera, Francisco Manrique. "Notas sobre la novela puertorriqueña de los últimos 55 años." *Asomante* (San Juan) 11 (1955): 24–28. Considers *The Blaze, Montoya Plantation,* and *The Undertow* as "the best trilogy of Laguerre." Brief commentary about *The 30th of February* and *The Fingers of the Hand* with provisional conclusions that in 1955 Laguerre "continues to be the only Puerto Rican novelist of significance and merit" rendering collective history with art and technical innovation.

González, José Emilio. *"Cauce sin río." Asomante* 19 (1963): 63–66. A critical appraisal briefly commenting upon characters and symbols with good observations on animal imagery and poetical regionalism.

———. *"El laberinto." Asomante* 16 (1960): 70–76. Largely summary and commentary about plot, expressing the critic's preference for interior perspective as in other Laguerre novels and for more local color in the Dominican Republic setting.

Martínez Capó, Juan. "La escena literaria; Enrique A. Laguerre: 'El fuego y su aire,' " *Puerto Rico Ilustrado* (supplement of *El Mundo*), August 15, 1961, p. 18. Brief but very incisive analysis of *Fire and Its Air* treating symbols of animalization and dehumanization, accumulation of mysteries, relation of form to content, and technical aspects. The critic calls this novel Laguerre's finest artistic achievement to date and convincingly shows why.

Martínez Nadal, Ernesto. "Consideraciones sobre la novela 'Cauce sin río' de Enrique A. Laguerre." *Revista del Instituto de Cultura Puertorriqueña* 7 (January–March 1964): 11–14. General observations about theme, possible message, and the universality of Puerto Rico's spiritual crisis. Notes Laguerre's attitude of tolerance toward characters.

Meléndez, Concha. *La generación del treinta: Cuento y novela.* San Juan: Instituto de Cultura Puertorriqueña, 1972, pp. 31–36. Brief but good overview of novels up to *The Ceiba Tree in the Flower Pot,* with some reference to symbols.

———. "El llamado de la montaña: Apuntes sobre la novela de Enrique A. Laguerre." In *Obras completas,* I, San Juan: Instituto de Cultura Puertorriqueña, 1970, 399–404. Notes on *The Blaze,* pointing out social and psychological themes and situating the novel within Spanish-American trends of the rural novel and proletarian art. The critic notes some affectation of style but is enthusiastic in her appraisal.

———. *"La resaca."* In *Obras completas,* II, 409–14. Fine discussion of the use of symbolism, metaphors, and images to clarify theme and define characters.

———. "*Solar Montoya,* novela de Enrique Laguerre." In *Obras completas,* II, 53–56. Good observations on *criollismo,* the development of Laguerre's prose style, and synthesis of Puerto Rican history in the novel.

Pedreira, Antonio A. "Prólogo a la segunda edición" of *La llamarada.* 19th ed. Barcelona: Ediciones Rumbos, 1968, pp. 5–11. Written in 1937, this prologue proclaims *The Blaze* a "great Puerto Rican novel," citing its artistic values, themes, and treatment of "spiritual crisis" reflecting the times. Discusses nature as protagonist, the central theme of the oppressive sugar cultivation, secondary themes of the life and psychology of country people, and the excellent development of introspection and action, launching a genuinely Puerto Rican art.

Rivera de Álvarez, Josefina. *Diccionario de la literatura puertorriqueña,* II. San Juan, Instituto de Cultura Puertorriqueña, 1974, 812–20. Excellent overview of Laguerre's life and works, with a brief evaluation mentioning salient points of each up to *The Labyrinth* and a very good bibliography.

Sánchez-Vilar, Isabel. "Los títulos en la novelística laguerriana." *Revista del Instituto de Cultura Puertorriqueña* (October–December 1967): 8–10. A brief but interesting consideration of the appropriateness and suggestiveness of the titles of Laguerre's novels. Implicit in the reading of this study is the fact that he obviously concedes great importance to finding a title which irradiates significance.

Vientós Gastón, Nilita. "La novela de Laguerre *La ceiba en el tiesto.*" *Índice cultural,* Vol. 50. Río Piedras: Ediciones de la Universidad de Puerto Rico, 1962, pp. 239–42. Comments upon the novel as a psychological study of a vacillating conscience which includes the great themes of the Puerto Rican novel: racial mixture, emigration, and nationalism. Finds the character of Julio Antonio a particularly fine creation of historical and individual conscience but criticizes the novel's covering too much territory in so few pages.

Index

The works of Laguerre are listed under his name.

Alegría, Ciro, 6
Alegría, Fernando, 8, 9, 22
Alegría, Ricardo, 137
Alonso, Manuel A., 27–28
Arce de Vázquez, Margot, 140
Arriví, Francisco, 80, 81, 95, 125, 130, 138, 139
Ashford, Bailey K., 35
Asturias, Miguel Ángel, 88
Ayala, Francisco, 45, 88

Baldorioty de Castro, Ramón, 74
Baroja, Pío, 22
Beauchamp, José Juan, 30, 80, 81, 82, 85
Belaval, Emilio S., 125
Benavente, Jacinto, 127
Betances, Ramón Emeterio, 119, 120
Biblical allusions, 39–40, 48–49, 68–69, 79, 97–98, 100, 107, 147, 155n3
Blasco Ibáñez, Vicente, 16
Borges, Jorge Luis, 14

Calderón de la Barca, Pedro, 48
Capetillo, Luisa, 54
Carpentier, Alejo, 117
Cela, Camilo José, 112
Cervantes, Miguel de, 45, 99; *Don Quijote de la Mancha*, 5, 21, 25, 41, 69, 70, 72, 144, 153n17
Coll, Edna, 117
Coll y Toste, Cayetano, 19
Compostela, (Francisco Vázquez Díaz), 103, 105, 140
Cordero Molina, Rafael, 74, 76, 154n18
Cortázar, Julio, 31, 117, 122
Cortés, Hernán, 21
Cotto-Thorner, Guillermo, 78

De Diego, José, 82, 136

Espronceda, José de, 96
Estébanez Calderón, Serafín, 27

Fable, *see* myth
Fernández Juncos, Manuel, 27
Forster, E. M., 112, 115
Fuentes, Carlos, 117

Galdós, *see* Pérez Galdós
Galíndez, Jesús de, 89–91
Gallegos, Rómulo, 5, 9, 16, 55, 127
García Márquez, Gabriel, 31, *117–18*
Geigel Polanco, Vicente, 4, 140

Index

Generation of the 1930s, 4, 25, 30, 32, 36, 61, 100, 117, 125, 141, 147
Gómez, Labor, 62, 64
Gómez Tejera, Carmen, 2
Granell, E. F., 88
Greco, El, 95–96
Greek tragedy, 129, 131
Güiraldes, Ricardo, 5, 9, 24, 25; *Don Segundo Sombra,* 22, 36

Hernández, José: *Martín Fierro,* 70, 75
Hostos, Eugenio María de, 92, 140
Hugo, Victor, 44, 99

Ibsen, Henrik, 127
Iglesias, Santiago, 54
Indice, 4, 137
Irony, 55–57, 90–92, 97–98, 104–105, 111, 113, 116, 128, 130, 132–33, 134, 135, 149

Jíbaro, 14–15, *24–41,* 130–31

Kierkegaard, Søren, 49

Laguerre, Enrique A.: as a young writer, 3–5; childhood, 1–3; pseudonyms, 135; readings, 4–5; teaching career, 2,4,5,7; travels, 5–6, 7

WORKS: ESSAYS
"Hojas libres" (Free Pages), 6, 144
Poesía modernista en Puerto Rico, La, (Modernist Poetry in Puerto Rico), 4, 65, 135–37
Polos de la cultura iberoamericana (Poles of Ibero-American Culture), 140–41
Pulso de Puerto Rico (Pulse of Puerto Rico), 6, 62, 64, 67, 95, 137–142

WORKS: NOVELS
Amos benévolos, Los (Benevolent Masters), 6, 8, 41, 53, *109–124,* 132, 147, 148, 149
Cauce sin río (River Bed without a River), 6, 7, 41, *93–100,* 103, 104, 132, 133, 146, 147, 148
Ceiba en el tiesto, La (The Ceiba Tree in the Flower Pot), 3, 40, *77–83,* 85, 87, 88, 95, 100, 135, 145, 147, 149
Dedos de la mano, Los (The Fingers of the Hand), 3, 40, 42, *50–57,* 81, 126, 133–34, 138, 139
Fuego y su aire, El (Fire and Its Air), 6, 8, 13, 41, 93, *100–108,* 138, 141, 147, 148, 149
Laberinto, El (The Labyrinth), 6, 40, 77, *84–94,* 103, 104, 140, 145, 148
Llamarada, La (The Blaze), 2, 3, 5, *9–23,* 26, 32, 40, 41, 45, 123–24, 127, 131, 132, 146, 148, 149
Resaca, La (The Undertow), 5, *58–76,* 104, 127, 135, 141, 145, 147, 148
Solar Montoya (Montoya Plantation), 2, 4, 5, *24–41,* 68, 127, 132, 133, 146, 147, 148
30 de febrero, El (The 30th of February), 4, 8, *42–50,* 79, 127, 132, 146

WORKS: SHORT STORIES
"Enemigo, El" (The Enemy), 131, *133–34*
"Naufragio" (Shipwreck), 131, *134–35*
"Pacholí," 131, *132–33*
"Raíces" (Roots), 131–32

WORKS: THEATER
Resentida, La (The Resentful Woman), 1, 5, *125–31*

Lares, 61
Lazarillo de Tormes, 115
Lloréns Torres, Luis, *136–37,* 140
Louis XIV, 113, 117, 123
Lope de Vega Carpio, Félix, 129

Machado, Antonio, 139
Manrique Cabrera, Francisco, 27, 140
Mármol, José, 88
Marqués, René, 80, 81, 138
Martínez Capó, Juan, 105–106
Meléndez, Concha, 4, 10, 19, 24 45, 60, 64, 66, 80, 133, 140
Melón, Esther M., 24
Mesonero Romanos, Ramón de, 27
Metaphor, 1, 19–21, 36, 41, 48, 52, 81–83, 96–99, 104–106, 111–17, 130, 139, 147–48
Morfi, Angelina, 58
Muñoz Marín, Luis, 4, 29, 65, 80, 81, 103–104, 138
Myth, 37–41, 44, 49–50, 67–70, 83, 85–87, 106–107, 119, 141, 147

Navarro Tomás, Tomás, 81

Oller, Francisco, 74
Ortega y Gasset, José, 13, 100

Palés Matos, Luis, 4–5
Pedreira, Antonio S., 4, 5, 9, 10, 12, 14, 17, 18, 24, 30, 123, 140
Pérez Galdós, Benito, 8, 55, 58, 60
Picaresque novel, 115
Ponce de León, Juan, 106, 107

Rechany Agrait, Luis, 141
Requena, Andrés, 88–90
Rincón de Gautier, Felisa, 103
Rivera, José Eustasio, 5, 9, 18, 22
Rodríguez Torres, Carmelo, 117

Salcedo, Diego, 60, 64
Sánchez, Luis Rafael, 117
Sanz, Gen. José Laureano, 62, 66, 73
Sarmiento, Domingo Faustino, 16 88
Sartre, Jean Paul, 115
Socialists, 10–11, 54
Soto, Pedro Juan, 117
Swift, Jonathan, 116–17
Symbolism, *See* metaphor

Taíno Indians, 15, 31, 32, 60, 63, 64, 68, 100, 106, 107, 135, 147
Tapia y Rivera, Alejandro, 74
Titles, 20, 36, 52, 64, 81, 85–86, 104, 105, 115, 119, 127, 147–48
Trujillo, Rafael Leonidas, *88–94,* 101, 102, 103, 107

Unamuno, Miguel de, 49
Urayoán (*see also* Uroyoán, Uroyán), 60, 63, 64, 68, 106, 135

Valle-Inclán, Ramón del, 88

Zayas Micheli, Luis O., 4, 10, 13, 15, 29, 31, 46, 55, 64, 69, 72, 80, 83, 100, 102, 119

Zeno Gandía, Manuel, 3, 10, 32, 33, *142–44*

THE LIBRARY
ST. MARY'S COLLEGE OF MARYLAND
ST. MARY'S CITY, MARYLAND 20686